D1032776

The Spirituality of the Layman

DESCLEE COMPANY, INC.

New York   Tournai   Paris   Rome

The Spirituality of the Layman

BY R. L. OECHSLIN, O. P.

Translated by Michael C. O'Brien

First published in French under the title *Une spiritualité des Laïcs*
(© 1963 by Editions Montaigne, Paris)

NIHIL OBSTAT
John A. Goodwine, J.C.D.
Censor Librorum

IMPRIMATUR
✠ Francis Cardinal Spellman
Archbishop of New York
August 19, 1964

© 1964 Desclee Co., Inc.
Library of Congress Catalog Card Number: 64–23932
Manufactured in the United States of America by
H. Wolff, New York

Contents

24345

The Spirituality of the Layman

Introduction

In our times, the Church is aware of a new birth. One of the most outstanding traits of this is the more vital awareness the entire Christian community has of the work of the Church, and in which they have an active part. Ours is the age of Catholic Action. Pius XI gave it its credentials as well as a decisive impetus. He was especially concerned with forming an elite corps of laymen who could penetrate their environment with the leaven of Christianity. We witnessed the birth and rapid growth of specialized movements, formed along the lines of the Young Christian Workers. Then, little by little, a broader concept of the lay apostolate developed during the pontificate of Pius XII. Indeed, this same Pope once remarked, "There has always been an apostolate of laymen in the Church of Christ." [1] But this apostolate involved certain personalities only, and not the generality of laymen.

The rise of the lay apostolate movement began in the sixteenth century. "It is since the Council of Trent that the laity has taken its place and progressed in apostolate activities." [2] Within the last thirty years, this idea has taken hold of the Christian people: "All are engaged, and today more than ever, in thinking not only of their own private needs in their prayers and sacrifices, but also of God's great designs in the world, in accord with the spirit of the *Our Father* which Jesus Christ Himself taught." [3] Also, six years later, at the Second World Congress of the Lay Apostolate, this same Pius XII was able to make a jubilant affirmation: "If today this awareness is awakened and if the term 'lay apostolate' is more frequently used when there is talk of the Church's activity, it is because the collaboration of the laity with the hierarchy was never so necessary, nor practiced in so systematic a way." [4]

Finally, the Second Vatican Council opened new perspectives to lay initiative. This great assembly of the Church could not be taken up by a hierarchy detached from the Christian people. Each of the faithful, whether cleric or lay, had to feel responsible. Two years before the first session of the Council, the bishops of Holland in a remarkable joint letter, after outlining the tasks the Council would have to take up, addressed this pressing appeal to the laity: "For this immense task, a general assembly of the world-wide episcopate could not suffice. It could give but a new impulse, an animation. The achievement of this gigantic work must come from the loyal fidelity and evangelical life of all Catholics." [5]

So the layman is more and more involved in the responsibility of the Church. The concept of a passively docile laity, a sort of flock under the direction of its leaders, has never been admitted in the teaching of the Church. If in practice we have come to the point where a large number of Christians act in such a manner, this attitude is today less acceptable than ever. The mission the Church received of carrying the light of truth to the world and of permeating the world with divine life has become a most urgent task. No Christian can divest himself of the duty to be a participant.

But if the need is so pressing and so far-reaching, the laity must find the means of facing it. As for the clergy, have they not too often been content with offering the layman only technical means? Would not a history of the twentieth-century Christian laity come down principally to describing the evolution of different formulas for the apostolate, one replacing another in the course of these past sixty or so years? We are anxious to find the right formula, and as soon as it has been used, we are in a hurry to propose another which will indeed be a novelty before it revolutionizes the methods of the apostolate and every other one becomes outdated.

It would be easy to illustrate this with a few concrete examples. We have seen the birth of Church guilds (as with Timon-David at Marseille), their brilliant rise, then their decline; the same for the Young Christian Workers and the other specialized movements which saw a rocket-like rise before becoming bogged down in technicalities. Then the trend was toward purely spiritual means. Groups like the Legion of Mary found more favor.

Far be it from us to discredit the different apostolic movements. This illustration is somewhat a caricature because we are emphasizing certain real traits. By no means should we reject techniques and methods. They are necessary. And it is fortunate that in our time much progress has been made in this field. By adapting apostolic action to the milieu we are going to approach, and by reflecting on the most suitable means, we marshal our forces; we render to the word of God a new power with which to permeate the world.

However, that is not the essential thing. Techniques are something like transmitting channels. If they have nothing to communicate, their perfection is useless. We repeat that apostolic action must flow from an authentic Christian life. There is no effective apostolate without personal fervor. But too often the laity are deprived of the very food of the interior life. Indeed the Church has always, in our own as in the first centuries, communicated light and life to every Christian. But general doctrine and the means offered to all is one thing; their adaptation to daily life and to each personal situation is quite another. Undoubtedly, this latter preoccupation predominated from the beginning. In fact, besides the elements of everyday catechesis which we can find throughout the New Testament,[6] we must also recognize in Saint Paul or in Saint John a personal way of living Christianity, what is called today one's own proper spirituality.

This is not the place to distinguish different types of spirituality, nor to discuss the very notion of spirituality. We leave this discussion to the next chapter. Recall but the appearance in the Church's history of great leaders who helped to adapt Christian doctrine to practical life.

The Church has not lacked such spiritual guides in the course of the centuries, but have they been directly concerned with the layman and his particular problems? Through the ages, the monastic life has remained the ideal of the fervent life underlying works of charity, even for Christians in the world. For example, the daily rule in the family of Jane Francis de Chantal was based on the horarium of a cloistered monastery. Again in the nineteenth century, the young Lacordaire gives the impression of having led, while with his mother, an austere life, one which cut him off from the world.[7]

The fact is, the layman is to remain in the world. He needs practices animated by a spirit that will help him permeate all his activities with an intense interior life, but which will leave him truly in the world and let him participate fully in the common life of men. Such was the orientation Francis de Sales gave his guidance when he advised Philothea to be always the best-dressed of her set.[8] About the same time, pious groups as well were looking for forms of the spiritual life suited to people in the world. Aside from the Company of the Blessed Sacrament, take for example the remarkable renovation by Father Michaelis of the Dominican Third Order at Toulouse.[9]

But, to speak of our times, we have progressed in this by giant strides. Secular institutes are a completely original innovation. They let one live according to the requirements of a life totally dedicated to God—justly called a state of perfection —but living fully the life of a layman in the world. Indeed, many more or less strict associations insist more and more on the lay character of their institution. To become aware of this, a glance at their publications suffices: bulletins of different Third Orders; *Act,* a C.F.M. monthly; *Action,* paper of the Y.C.W.

Hence, for the laity, a complete literature of spirituality containing many riches has arisen and developed. On the other hand, a variety of books on one point or another of the Christian life have appeared, aimed especially at the laity. Note, for example, the excellent work of Lebret and Suavet: *An Examination of Conscience for Modern Catholics.*[10]

The role of the layman in the Church is equally the object of important studies in theology. It is hardly useful to name them since they are already widely known, e.g., *Lay People in the Church* by Yves Congar.

As to these last works, they are based on the plane of theological principles and not on the practical level of the Christian's life in the world. Thus the need to make a transition or adaptation remains before we can speak of spirituality.

On the other side, the publications of various lay spiritual movements are especially concerned with spirituality. Nevertheless, whether we envision a Christian life inspired by the spiritual principles of a certain religious society (as the Third Orders), or whether we emphasize a particular aspect of Christian life (for example, the spirituality of marriage or marital devotion), we do not yet have a unified picture.

The task yet remains of presenting a synthetic view of the spirit in which the layman in the world should live his Christian life.

The layman lives in the world. In it he accomplishes certain tasks willed by God. Various means are at his disposal. It is with this situation that lay spirituality is concerned. To characterize it, we must determine those tasks which belong properly to the layman; we must determine exactly the conditions of his life with relation to the world; finally we must understand how, in his role as layman, he must use the means for grace given to every Christian. Then it will be possible to determine the position of the layman in Christ's Mystical Body. Many chapters will be dedicated to these different questions.

This task is vast. Should one wish to fill it completely and develop all its aspects, it would require a thick tome on the spiritual life. The research, both in the realm of doctrine, and on the practical applications, is not sufficiently advanced. An endeavor of this sort would be premature. We will give here but an outline. Our task is above all to put in focus the central perspective, that of the *consecration of the world* by and in the sacrifice of Christ. Then we can attempt to map out some further approaches.

Certain fields are already the object of numerous publications; we do not believe it useful to develop these here—such as the field of prayer or the spirituality of marriage.

Before setting out on our subject, we must ask the preliminary question, for all discussion would be in vain without first resolving it. Does there exist a spirituality proper to the layman, and what, first of all, do we mean by spirituality? There is a good deal of disagreement on these two points.

However, since they are closely linked to each other, we shall treat them together in the first chapter.

FOOTNOTES:

[1] Discourse to the Second World Congress of the Lay Apostolate, October 5, 1957. Cf. Cattin-Conus, *Sources de la Vie spirituelle,* Fribourg, 1958–61, II, n. 4350.

[2] Discourse to the First World Congress of the Lay Apostolate, October 14, 1951. Cf. Cattin-Conus, *ibid.,* II, n. 4274.

[3] Cattin-Conus, *loc. cit.,* II, n. 4281.

[4] *Ibid.,* n. 4350.

[5] *Doctrine catholique,* 68 (1961), col. 797.

[6] Cf. Jean Daniélou, *Message évangélique et Culture hellénistique aux IIe et IIIe siècles,* Tournai, 1961, pp. 147–184.

[7] P. Baron, *La Jeunesse de Lacordaire,* Paris, 1961, pp. 30–32.

[8] *Introduction to the Devout Life,* III, ch. 25.

[9] "Un foyer d'apostolat dominicain au XVIIe siècle," *Vie Dominicaine,* Fribourg, 20 (1961), pp. 25–31.—This Fraternity constituted a center of spiritual life where persons of every rank kept close together, bringing their light to the city in the form of works of charity, some very daring.

[10] For those who read French, we might mention also the collection *Spiritualité* put out by the Editions Ouvrières, and the excellent work of Ivan Gobry, *La pauvreté du laïc,* Paris, 1961.

1

Is There a Spirituality
of the Layman?

Many have already answered "yes" to this question. They speak
of a spirituality of the laity and even distinguish various types
within it. They associate these types with different Catholic
Action movements or with certain modes of Christian life.
And so they distinguish a spirituality of the laborer, of the
family, of scouts, etc.

We can't examine all the attempts made along this line in
our day, but we must ask ourselves if their aim was valid and
if they offer us a solid starting point.

Father Louis Bouyer thinks this is indeed a mistake: "Coming finally to the various forms of spirituality for workers,
farmers, students, etc., which have been proposed in certain
circles of specialized Catholic action, we find that there seems
to be a confusion here between the legitimate concern that the
spirituality of the Gospel should permeate the solutions to
problems proper to each particular environment, and a vague
and chimerical ideal which, if it were (or could be) defined,
would come down to refashioning the Gospel to fit the mentality, the professional bent, the prejudices or the current fads
of one or another of these various environments. . . . At this

rate, we should speedily arrive at the production of a Christianity, or rather of a multitude of Christianities, of classes or cliques, of the kind at which Saint Paul's exclamation is directly aimed: 'There is no longer either Greek or Jew, either circumcision or uncircumcision, either Barbarian or Scythian, either slave or free man, but Christ is all in all' (Col. 3, 11)." [1]

Perhaps this condemnation is rather abrupt. To clarify our judgment, we might examine how we have come to recognize these varieties of lay spirituality.

Indeed, they seem to be conceived analogically with the spiritualities of religious orders. In fact, we often hear mention of a Benedictine, Franciscan, Dominican, Carmelite, Ignatian spirituality, and so on. [2] We would think that an examination of the type that served as model might shed some light on the picture. Unfortunately, it only adds to the confusion.

First, there is no agreement on the criteria for distinguishing one spirituality from another. Thus, while one man reduces the different spiritualities to the smallest possible number, another multiplies them without limit. And there are many opinions between these two extremes.

Some imagine an absolute dichotomy. They base this on whether the spiritual families stress this point or that: love or sacrifice; [3] personal effort or grace; [4] theocentric or anthropocentric orientation, [5] and to this last some add a third category of Christocentric orientation. [6]

The opposite camp tends to multiply spiritualities. Fr. Heerinckx, [7] for example, claims there are eleven schools of spirituality: monastic, oriental, Benedictine, Carthusian, Dominican, Franciscan, that of the *devotio moderna,* Ignatian, Carmelite, Salesian, Berullian and Liguorian. But in this division, the distinguishing principles are rather obscure.

This approach tends to a special spirituality for each congregation and each saint, and so justifies Father Bouyer's protests.[8]

Our rapid foray into these different classifications should not discourage us. Some fallacy of method must lie at the root of this confusion, and it is not hard to discover. We use the word spirituality without clearly defining it. More precisely, we began by using it in too narrow a sense without realizing it. Later we find it impossible to arrange certain aspects of reality in so poorly constructed a category. Because of this, the word has changed meanings in the course of centuries. For example, take the article *Ecole de spiritualité* by Father Lucien-Marie in the *Dictionnaire de spiritualité.*[9] The entire treatment is excellent and certainly inspiring. However, in the course of the article we pass surreptitiously from the expression "school of spirituality" to the simple word "spirituality." We come away with the impression that these terms are equivalent.[10] The definition of "school of spirituality" is quite clear: it is "the particular system in which certain groups or certain ages present the spiritual path which leads the soul to God."[11] But indeed, "spirituality" has a very different meaning, a meaning which goes far beyond that of "school." We can live a spirituality without reflecting on its nature, without making a theory of it, without making it into a system.

There is an historical explanation for this change of meaning. The present notion of spirituality depends upon an entire spiritual movement dating from the fifteenth and sixteenth centuries. The men of that age reflected upon the interior acts which are implied in the soul's ascent toward God. They created a system along these lines and centered it especially on prayer. This is not surprising, for the religious institutions born or developing at that time were also stressing prayer for a number of reasons. On the one hand, reacting to religious formalism, the Protestant reformers were insisting on interior religion. In this respect, they were answering a true need of the soul. But Catholics were not lacking to satisfy this same need. There were powerful spiritual currents in various parts of Europe, notably in the Low Countries, in the Rhineland of the fourteenth century, and also in Italy. The Humanists too were interested in these questions of the interior life, among them Erasmus. There was a mystic invasion, with certain traces of illuminism, in sixteenth-century Spain. This activity in Spain included not only the Carmelite reform carried out by Saint Teresa and Saint John of the Cross, but also the spiritual renewals which marked the other orders: the Franciscans, the Dominicans and the Augustinians.[12] Then too, new religious societies were forming, striving to give their members greater freedom of action in order to meet successfully the necessities of the contemporary apostolate. They freed themselves from the traditional framework of the monastic life, the liturgical office and the cloister, and the core of their spiritual life tended to become purely internal. This required a systematic ordering of the interior life. The Nordic spiritual current, called the *devotio moderna,* came to the fore with its arsenal of prayers and other methodic exercises.[13]

The combination of all these factors led men to see the spiritual path of the soul toward God as uniquely internal and rigorously mapped out according to a definite system. If we say that a spirituality is the concrete system of approaching God, we are thereafter completely occupied with the conscious and systematic manner of approaching God in prayer. These ideas are so deeply rooted in the mind of the author of a recent book that, desiring to give a general appraisal of the different ways of looking at spirituality, he concluded by writing: "The history of spirituality coincides substantially with the history of prayer." [14]

Certainly this idea of spirituality is too narrow. Its insufficiency tends—as we shall see—to neglect certain important psychological factors. If, on the contrary, we give the idea of spirituality its complete meaning, we have to admit the existence of a spirituality of the layman.

Take this as a tentative definition: spirituality is a man's concrete way of going to God. This amounts to what Pius XII said: "The spirituality of a saint is his particular way of picturing God, of speaking about Him, of approaching Him, of dealing with Him." [15] The soul does not go to God alone, as if man were a pure spirit. The soul is an incarnate spirit; it is the *form* of the body. It permeates it so profoundly that it spiritualizes it. The activities of the body in turn reveal the spirit. Actions, movements, attitudes, even one's whole life have a special meaning. Because of our relations with God, our life has a religious meaning. Therefore spirituality is not concerned with interior prayer alone, but involves man's total behavior throughout every instant of daily life.

Let's look at some expressions closely related to the word "spirituality": "to act with a certain spirit," "to be in good or bad spirits." Now take the example of a child in school. A certain spiritual significance and value inspires his conduct, his attitude, his activities with others. He adds nothing material to them, but he gives them a particular meaning. Even if he says nothing, his entire behavior conveys a special meaning. In the realm of spirituality, the Church offers a divine framework. This is the place to bring in the notion of vocation, as Fr. Bouyer fortunately does: "Yet to the diversity of persons and their situations correspond different types of vocations, different forms of life proposed by the same grace to one and another for the same purpose. It might even be said that every vocation is, in a sense, individual, as every person, every human destiny, is unique and irreplaceable. There are, nonetheless, different families of 'charisms,' different fundamental forms which grace may come to take among mankind, by which the same Spirit works differently in all the members for the good of the one body which they form together in the whole Christ." [16]

An important role has been given to the natural conditions of life in attempts to characterize a spirituality. Fr. Lucien-Marie expresses these natural conditions as "the *terrain* in which the essential rhythm (of the spiritual life) is actualized." [17] He adds, "There are natural substructures, both conscious and unconscious, within each individual, as there are in society, and society and the individual influence each other profoundly. Now the role of these natural substructures in the *differentiations* of schools of spirituality is very important. Among these, temperament, character, personal history, and sociological coordinates are so many given factors which have always played a part in the history of spirituality. . . . In the concrete, that is in the actual order (not in the theoretical or abstract order), we can pose these as the source of the differentiations. This reality of the individual and collective terrain determines not only the often-intuitive choice of one spirituality rather than another, but to a great extent explains the origin and evolution of the spiritual currents in the Church's life." [18]

We must go even further than this author. We are not concerned with a "material factor" only, but with an incarnate spirit or the spiritualization of social behavior. We often rely too much on a conception which cuts man in half, a dichotomy between body and soul. Man is more *one* than we imagine. His simple act may express a thought as clearly as the most explicit word. The presence of the spirit does not depend upon words or explicit representation. Often a movement of the hand or wrinkling of the brow contains a message and takes the place of speech. The more complex the attitude and the more it involves the whole man, the more capable it is of communicating the spirit. There are also ways of acting in a religious context. "Observances" can be charged with spirituality. A procession, genuflections, hands elevated and joined do not need words to explain that they signify prayer. If we do not stop at the "form" of life implied by the free acceptance of the vows, and if we consider the whole man, we can recognize a spiritual force of the highest nature acting throughout all human behavior.

In the above cases we have been talking about social dynamisms, technically called *habitus,* which the Church offers to a group of men or to all Christians. These give a certain orientation to the soul. They are a framework of life to support the spirit. Indeed this is the way the Holy Spirit inspires the Christian community and marks it with His seal. But this inspiration has to be accepted. If we consider these Christian observances or practices simply as limitations to free and individual initiative, they become obstacles, they seem purely material and devoid of all spiritual meaning.

To illustrate this, we might consider a religious order. A certain spirit guides the life of each of the members. Is it not evident that this determines each member's very own way of life in his approach to God? Is his life not shaped by the supple framework which envelops the community? There is the particular chapel with its definite liturgy; there is the cloister, a place conducive to silence and meditation; there is the solemn rite of meals, the distribution of different daily jobs, the very rhythm of life. All these things unify life and direct it toward a single purpose, the very purpose which the order in question pursues. This life permeates the members of the order much more than a spiritual system or a progressive method of prayer could ever do. If we were to look to the founder of this way of life, we would find a strong religious personality who was able to set up a more or less new social organization according to an original inspiration. His was an inspiration received from God and confirmed by the Church.

Each time we encounter the religious organization of the life of a determined social group, we can speak of a determined spirituality. But this can be true only to the degree in which its dynamics can involve all the person's activities. And so we can speak of an Ignatian spirituality, a Benedictine spirituality, or a Dominican spirituality. But in the strict sense, we cannot speak of a "conjugal spirituality," because the purpose of marriage cannot direct all of man's activities. Many professional, civic, and cultural activities would be beyond its scope.

But these diverse types of spirituality are not completely independent of one another; they border one another, and the spiritual currents of history modify them all. Each is built around a solid and lasting core. In a religious order the rule and the constitution form this core, but even that can evolve under the influence of jurisprudence.

There is also a lay spirituality of this type. As Christians, the laity have received a vocation to divine life. They must pursue this vocation. And the Church provides a special spiritual framework suited to the role of men in the world. They have not received a special consecration to diffuse the means of salvation in the exercise of their particular functions in the Mystical Body. They do not bind themselves with public vows. Their role in the Mystical Body is distinct from that of clerics and religious. Because of this participation in the Mystical Body, their Christian life is developed in a particular way. We must define this role in relation to the vital center of this body, Christ its head who offers Himself in sacrifice. They participate in the salvation of the world by fulfilling their temporal commitment. By the very fact that they are laymen, the instruments of salvation—the sacraments, and the simple virtuous Christian life have a special meaning. Finally, the Church offers them foundations of life, special spiritual helps to sustain their Christian life in the world. This whole complexus, both spiritual and corporal, temporal but with eternal significance, gives the spirituality of the layman its character.

To make precise the way in which the laity are to respond to their particular vocation, we must first relate this vocation to the general vocation of mankind. This we shall do in the following chapter.

FOOTNOTES:

[1] Louis Bouyer, *Introduction to Spirituality,* New York: Desclée, 1961, p. 22.

[2] Cf. Jean Gautier, *Some Schools of Catholic Spirituality,* New York: Desclée, 1959.

[3] A. Tanquerey, *The Spiritual Life,* Tournai: Desclée, 1930.

[4] F. X. Maquart, "Causerie sur les revues: Ecoles de spiritualité," *La Vie spirituelle* (June 1926), pp. 310–334.

[5] H. Bremond, *A Literary History of Religious Thought in France,* London, 1930, *passim.*

[6] P. C. Cantini, "Le Scuole cattoliche di spiritualità," *La Scuola cattolica* (1950), pp. 103–125.

[7] *Introductio in Theologiam spiritualem,* Turin, 1931, p. 70.

[8] *Ibid.,* p. 22.

[9] *Dictionnaire de spiritualité,* Paris, 1960, IV, cols. 116–128.

[10] *Ibid.,* col. 117, 1°.

[11] *Ibid.,* col. 116.

[12] Cf. R. L. Oechslin, *Louis de Grenade ou la rencontre avec Dieu,* Paris, 1951, *passim.*

[13] Cf. the *Rosetum exercitiorum spiritualium* . . . of John Monbaer. V. Pierre Debongnies, *Jean Monbaer de Bruxelles, abbé de Livry, ses écrits et ses réformes,* Louvain, 1928.

[14] I. Colosio, *Saggi de Spiritualità domenicana,* Florence, 1961, p. 19.

[15] Discourse to the Franciscan Tertiaries of Italy, July 1, 1956. Cattin-Conus, *Sources de la Vie spirituelle,* II, n. 4246.

[16] L. Bouyer, *op. cit.,* p. 163.

[17] Fr. Lucien-Marie, "Ecole de spiritualité," *Dictionnaire de spiritualité,* IV, col. 118.

[18] *Ibid.,* cols. 118–119.

2

Conquest and Consecration
of the World

God calls men to a vocation according to the loving plan He
has for creation. This same vocation includes the lay vocation
and determines the spirit in which the layman should live.

Hear how Saint Paul expresses this vocation of man:
"Blessed be the God and Father of Our Lord Jesus Christ, who
has blessed us with every spiritual blessing on high in Christ.
Even as He chose us in Him before the foundation of the
world, that we should be holy and without blemish in His
sight in love." [1] The plan of God then is that man enter and
live forever in the divine mystery of love. But this approach
to God which supposes holiness—this sort of setting apart from
the world, this belonging to the sacred domain which is that
of the Most High—is not completed immediately at the instant
of creation. We can see the plan of God clearly enough in
the first pages of the Bible: man must develop himself from
the first moment of his existence, until he reaches the end
fixed by God. Living creatures are to grow according to the
divine benediction.[2] Loving holiness and perfect purity in the
presence of God the Father are perfected only at the end of
the period of earthly life.

Suffice it to say that all human life is directed to final joy. In fact, this final goal gives life all its value and its light. It is like a road which each one must travel. At the horizon where the road is lost, a brightness, like breaking dawn, marks its outline. Of course, the road runs here and there, rises and falls, disappears, then becomes visible again, but the light shines always for him who looks for it.

This light is the unshakable hope of attaining the intimate life with God which He has prepared for us. This hope is deeply rooted in our present life. For all the created good we enjoy here below reveals, by its very existence, the total reality and is a foretaste of this reality. Hope, then, makes us strive confidently in spite of all obstacles for the perfection of our being: our desires fulfilled beyond measure, our insatiable need to know satisfied by a penetrating look into the divine abyss where all good, all beauty, all happiness are found. The love which binds us one to another is being perfected by the union of us all and the union of God, who is all, with all of us in eternal love. To sum it up, eternal happiness is found in the personal God, three and one, whose love called us into existence, and in whom is found the fulfillment of that creative love. "We see now through a mirror in an obscure manner, but then face to face. Now I know in part, but then I shall know even as I have been known." [3]

Saint Paul is not speaking only of a vision and possession of God in the future. In this very earthly existence, we receive divine life like a seed God plants in the soul. The figure of the seed rightly suggests that something must receive it. Divine life permeates the whole human being; it assimilates him; it transforms him. Baptism begins this divine action; it "buries us in the death" of Christ that we may "rise with Him unto newness of life," [4] that is to say, to "put on Christ." [5] And so our activity becomes Christ's activity. Thus, through the development of human life, the divine life increases. An attraction is born in the depths of the soul, a secret desire to act in the manner of Jesus, and little by little we become more virtuous. We act with the kindness and humility of Christ, with His strength and His zeal and His charity. We become Christ-like. Life in society, the communion of men among themselves, these things become an image of the unity of the three persons in the Holy Trinity. The more we accept this to be an interior attraction, the more we experience a foretaste of eternal happiness. We begin to experience the Lord's goodness. We experience His goodness, His beauty, His joy, not outside ourselves, but in the very action accomplished under His influence. This experience is personal but it also lies at the heart of relationships between persons arising from love. The purer the love, the greater the experience. We seize the divine love as it were on the sly, in an instant which vanishes, only to be reborn in a new instant of grace.

We have said that the divine life develops in the midst of human existence. There are many facets to this human existence, nor can it develop properly without an evolution of the entire universe. Man's role involves all of creation; God's call to man is an appeal to realize a grandiose plan. God placed man in the world and placed in man powerful instincts for acting upon his environment. Secret energies would lead him to the conquest of this world, thus bringing him to a certain terrestrial happiness, and finally procure for him final fulfillment in the eternal mystery of divine perfection. The world does not exist solely to give man the ability to concretize his thoughts and ideas and make them precise. It is a mysterious domain which holds hidden treasures. He must labor hard to bring these treasures to light. Curiosity and the desire for happiness are incessant stimulants which give no rest to his heart.

God has placed His seal of approval on this good interior impulse by making man's task explicit. We find the divine command in Genesis presented from the beginning in picturesque formulas. Let man receive dominion over the world. Under God, he shall be its master, as God is the supreme Master: "Let us make mankind in our image and likeness; and let them have dominion over the fishes of the sea, the birds of the air, the cattle, over all the wild animals and every creature that crawls on the earth." [6] Man, by his activity, is to maintain and develop the order put by God into the universe: "The Lord God took the man and placed him in the garden of Eden to till it and to keep it." [7]

Even if in the beginning work was not difficult and unattractive as it was after the fall, it remained no less a rude task and required all man's energies to take it up and bring it to completion. But that is what gives it its value. If all the gifts of God, meanings and forces contained in nature, with their capacities to be signs and ways of access to the divine mystery, if all beauty, goodness, and truth were found always in the open, man would have no challenge and no appreciation. He would be like the rich man whose house was filled with jewels, but who was oblivious of their value, because an army of slaves brought him heaps of them. But nothing is of worth to a person, to a free being, except that which he has sought after, discovered, conquered. Work is a kind of creation. Thus God placed man in a world of innumerable energies and mysteries hidden under sensible forms, buried in the depths of celestial space, as well as at the center of the infinitely small atom. He endowed man with the capacities required to open, little by little, these secrets and by this very action to become great and powerful. God, in offering all this to man, has magnanimously given him a part of His creative power.

Behold man standing before creation. He sees this multitude of beings, from the inanimate to the most active and intricate living beings. His imagination suggests to him a multitude of ways in which to consider exterior objects. It dissociates them, brings them together again, gives birth to the most unexpected forms. Thus he develops a world of thoughts and sentiments in his soul. In addition, his hand comes to the aid of his intelligence: man makes new objects; his active intervention in creation releases new forces and new beings. He develops new ideas which emerge from the encounter between his action and inert or living realities. Because man is part of society, these thoughts and activities, developed from contact with nature, again multiply. For society implies personal encounters among men, and reciprocal exchanges, when based on love, increase man's power to discover and sharpen his discernment.

And so man uses all the powers of his being to shape the world. He brings to light a thousand reflections of beauty and truth, and these become his good. They increase him, and make him better to the degree that this good takes its rightful place in human life. This explains the secret delight of the soul at the sound of a marvelous symphony, or the joyous thrill at the sight of some masterpiece, or the enthusiasm of crowds who glorify the scientist for developing an atomic engine for the conquest of space, or simply the charm of beauty revealed to the senses and the pure joy of knowing.

These experiences constitute approaches to happiness. But the enjoyment they give soon becomes bitter if these things lead to nothing further. All beauty, all created truth should stir from a sap which is hidden at first, but which will soon push forth the new buds and flowers, culminating in the fruits of eternity. For example, how deceiving is the beauty of the body, perfect as it may be, if it harbors not an authentic love which implies a mutual gift and a mutual fulfillment in a greater than itself! How explain the infatuation of innumerable youths for some movie star, if not by a profoundly human instinct, the grand ideal of a perfect body? But if the exterior masks the lack of all spiritual reality, what final disgust and what depression! Similarly, the powerful instruments of science ought to be at the service of man, permitting him to live more fittingly, and enabling him to develop his spiritual faculties. What despair, on the contrary, when they are turned against man to crush him!

However, there is still more. According to God's plan, man's entire life here below should be at the same time divine life, a participation in the mystery of the Trinity. Therefore every human act is meant to be elevated, supernaturalized. A contemplation of creation which does not lead to God is unfulfilled; a love which stops exclusively at the creature is disfigured; an action limited to the conquest of the world is truncated. If, then, we examine the life of man at the instant of creation, we see that he had to grow by raising this temporal life through the use of creatures to the victory of eternal happiness. The first man realized a fully human life, discovering all the treasures of beauty and goodness of this world; and this life was an instrument of the celestial life already begun. In each of the creatures he encountered, man saw a manifestation of the beauty and goodness of all God's perfections, of a God who willed to be man's friend.

Creation was holy in the beginning. Though it had not yet reached its fulfillment, it was in perfect submission to God. Everything had its own natural reality and served to lead man to God. All the creatures of this world were submissive to man, and he advanced with creation toward the final goal of eternal happiness.

Sin destroyed this primitive harmony. It split the universe. From then on, the realities of nature were shut up in themselves. If order were to be reestablished, they had to be opened again to the supernatural, and this was possible only through an influx of divine life. The redemption is this work of restoration. Christ reconciles all things in Himself. Because He is the second Adam, He is the Leader of the new humanity; and since man received from God dominion over creation, He is Himself the King of the universe. This is to say that He makes His divine life as Son permeate regenerated humanity. He reintroduces the created world into the divine by His sacrifice: "And I, if I be lifted up from the earth, will draw all things to Myself." [8]

We rediscover here a primary principle of the divine plan: God does not impose His benefits on men. He wants man himself freely to attain his destiny. God gives all to man; nevertheless, man can take up this divine gift on his own account and act as a free person. Thus Christ, Head of the new humanity, the Mystical Body, won complete redemption once and for all, but the members must accept it and transmit it to all creatures. This restoration becomes a new and Christian conquest of the world. It is a work entirely centered in Christ. Christ is the overflowing source whence comes all life: He is the Alpha. Christ is also the goal which draws every creature to its perfection in Him: He is the Omega. And between these two poles is accomplished the redemption, the restoration of every creature in the mystery of the Lord.

Every Christian, since he is a member of Christ's body, is equipped to accomplish this work of restoration. Every creature, shut up in itself by sin, has been rejected from the divine domain, has become *profane*. Now it must be reintroduced into the divine, it must be *consecrated* to God.

Certainly this task of consecration requires the special vocations of the priest and of the religious. These we shall discuss later. But there is a general vocation of all mankind which comes before these special vocations. Little by little, man must bring each creature in his care into the domain of the All-holy God. This vocation concerns every man who lives in the common condition of men in the environment of this created world. The Christian who has a role in response to this vocation but is not called to one of the special vocations which we mentioned, is designated by the name of layman. Let us be content, for the moment, to use this word "layman" without making its meaning more precise. We leave that to a future chapter. From the point of view of his essential relationship to God, the layman's task is to consecrate the world to God. Pius XII recalled this in his discourse to the Second World Congress of the Lay Apostolate: "The *consecratio mundi* is essentially the work of laymen themselves, for they are intimately involved in economic and social life, they participate in government and in legislative assemblies." [9]

This is in accord with the plan of God which remains unchanged in spite of sin. Man's dominion over the world was not taken away. Although the curse of sin had affected all nature, man's task was still to develop by work. "Cursed be the ground because of you; in toil shall you eat of it all the days of your life." [10] We find the commandment to develop the order of the world repeated to man after the fall just as before the fall: "Therefore the Lord God put him out of the garden of Eden to till the ground from which he was taken." [11]

But human activity somehow had changed. It became uninviting. Man labored in suffering. He won his bread "by the sweat of his brow." Thus sin introduced suffering and separations. Thus there is one aspect we should not forget when we characterize the spirituality of laymen: that of sacrifice. It must suffice to note it, for we cannot develop this aspect to the full here. To see its full import, we must relate it to the sacrifice of Christ.

What perhaps appears immediately clear is that the conquest of the world has become a most arduous task. Man is the summit of the hierarchy of worldly organization, and creatures should turn spontaneously through him to God. But creatures are now shut up in themselves, turned not to God but to themselves. Each tends to become a center in a generalized anarchy. If we are to restore order through a total unity in Christ by "putting on Christ," the second Adam, we have to realize first that the primitive order of the world was, so to say, already vested in the first Adam. Adam was the summit of the human hierarchy, as now Christ is the Head of the new hierarchy which forms His body. All the forces of nature tended to harmony in this organization headed by Adam. Their inclinations rendered them docile to the lord of the earth.

This same order has to be reestablished. Thus man has a double task in all his actions. The primitive instincts to live and develop remain deeply rooted in his heart, responding interiorly to the command of God who imposes on man the task of conquering the world. He must use these human powers not only for the spontaneous and joyful opening of nature to bring to light its hidden treasures, but also for the hard encounter, the physical battle, to reestablish man's dominion over nature. This double action on the world has its parallel on the spiritual plane too. More precisely, it should bring about a new influx of divine life into every creature. We said earlier that every human act is to be elevated, supernaturalized. This is still true, but there is now a medicinal aspect, because the world has been dislocated, dissociated, wounded by sin. This medicinal aspect is very crucial in the layman's task in the world. But this task is being accomplished in Christ in accordance with God's plan.

When we speak of the consecration of the world, to this last word we must give a very wide meaning. There is the world completely exterior to man. This includes the material objects which he uses: those which serve for daily life—food, clothes, and the satisfaction of immediate necessities—or even all the numerous and ever more advanced technical instruments which let him accomplish more work with less effort. We can also include here the more and more effective organizational methods he uses. But the more man extends his power by science and technology, the more he risks deceiving himself and organizing the world without God. This makes us realize the importance of the Christian's making the necessary adjustments.

We must take into account the social world too. It is, in fact, closely linked to the physical world. The scientific organization of the world determines certain economic conditions and certain forms of life in society. Laws and social relationships determine and limit this complexus. Here too is an immense domain for the Christian spirit to penetrate and little by little divinize.

Finally, we must guard against establishing an absolute separation between the body or even the whole man and exterior objects. The senses perceive the world as outside the body. Yet this world extends man's members and his diverse human powers or faculties. With the telescope or television, the eye extends its visual horizon beyond the immediate; with the electric brain, intelligence multiplies its organizational power. But inversely, the exterior world deeply influences the powers of the soul by acting through the body. Who would deny, for example, that man's feelings are influenced by the movies he watches? In addition, there is a completely undisciplined world within man. That world also he must order and more and more perfectly consecrate to God by the powers of his intellect and will.

Through all human activity, man realizes the task of consecrating the world by influencing the external world and the world within himself. His actions realize a progressive conquest stimulated by the natural instincts which drive him to live and to develop, thus realizing a progressive conquest of the world. These profound tendencies support his efforts, and reflection directs and organizes them. Thus, our civilization gradually develops with all its advances in the domains of art, literature, science, and of social, economic, and political organizations.

By that fact, each one finds himself in a concrete situation with diverse means for action upon himself and upon those around him. That is where the task of man lies: throughout his life he must develop his capacities to the maximum, profit from the talents received from God, and draw into this growth the creatures around him.

It is in this human task itself that man accomplishes the consecration of every creature to God. By acting with all the perfection possible on the human level, he sanctifies the world. In this way—through human action—the world passes in stages into the domain of God.

FOOTNOTES:

[1] Eph. 1, 3–4.
[2] Cf. Gn. 1, 28.
[3] 1 Cor. 13, 12.
[4] Cf. Rom. 6, 4.
[5] Cf. Rom. 13, 14.
[6] Gn. 1, 26.

[7] Gn. 2, 15.

[8] Jn. 12, 32.

[9] Cattin-Conus, *Sources de la Vie spirituelle,* II, n. 4313.

[10] Gn. 3, 17.

[11] Gn. 3, 23.

3

Commitment of the Layman
and Separation from the World

The world we must consecrate to God is the world corrupted by sin. It can no longer be approached as the world in the state of innocence, for it conceals traps and allurements. Therefore, in dealing with it we must keep our distance and maintain a certain separation between ourselves and the world. We realize that the consecration of the world envisions the entry of creatures into the divine world. Therefore, to accomplish this task, we must first belong to God. Separation from the world implies reserving a certain sacred domain to God, where His mystery resides, well protected. From this domain the divine power has to illumine the world, attract it, transform it and, finally, assimilate it.

In fact, throughout the history of salvation, whenever God calls man to work for the restoration of the world wounded by sin, He demands of him a separation. This began with Abraham, the father of the Chosen People: "Leave your country, your kinsfolk and your father's house, for the land which I will show you,"[1] Yahweh said to him. Thereafter he will have to live at odds with the idolatrous milieu surrounding him. He will remain in a certain intimacy with the Lord, an intimacy founded on a covenant, an intimacy so great that God will confide His projects to him and even permit him to dispute them with Him. This is the case in the admirable dialogue over the destruction of Sodom.[2] It is also the case with Jacob during the calamities which followed his disputes with his brother, Esau. His prolonged exile, at first simply a physical separation, became, under the persevering action of God, a very real setting apart and sanctification confirmed by his new name, "Israel," "strong against God."[3] The circumstances of Joseph's separation are even more dramatic. His prison became a privileged place where God blessed him with graces and prepared him to save his brothers in spite of their injustice: "Do not be distressed nor angry with yourselves that you sold me here; for God sent me before you to save (your) life. . . . God sent me before you to preserve a remnant for you in the land, and to deliver you in a striking way. Not you but God sent me here."[4]

However, the separation is much more marked with regard to the Chosen People. The exodus from Egypt is surely a liberation from slavery. Yet when they underwent the trials, hunger and thirst in the desert, these people yearned for the pleasures and joys they had known, and they murmured against Moses.[5] The halting, uncertain march across the desert was itself a test. Each incident preserved and strengthened their dependence on Yahweh, who sealed His dominion over them with a solemn covenant that left no doubt about His intent: "Therefore, if you harken to My voice and keep My covenant, you shall be My special possession, dearer to Me than all other people, though all the earth is Mine. You shall be to Me a kingdom of priests, a holy nation."[6]

Then come the prophets. Their mission was to make this separation interior and spiritual. What good are walls of stone and guarded frontiers that keep the godless peoples out if pagan ways creep in unchallenged? We must reject all this corruption and live a new life as a people on the march toward the Promised Land. The ideal of the desert haunts the prophets' imagination. Osee announces the restoration of this ideal, putting these words on the lips of Yahweh: "So I will allure her; I will lead her into the desert and speak to her heart." [7] Once more events will be the instrument of Providence. The people are led into exile. Under the blow of this trial, an elite is formed, stimulated by the prophets, an elite which will constitute a solid core when they set about restoring the nation after the return to the land of Israel. A considerable development of the cult of the law, after the exile and especially from the time of the Maccabees, soon leads to accentuation of the separation of the Jews from the pagans who surround them. But, principally among the Pharisees, the intimacy with God, which ought to guarantee this separation, is lost. Even communities like that of Qumran, living in the desert in total separation from the world, seem not to have been sheltered from juridical formalism.

Christ would restore the essential values with the foundation of His kingdom. This kingdom seems very mysterious; nevertheless it possesses a structure with a leader and members. Jesus is at the center; through Him we arrive at the domain of God; we sense here the presence and action of the Almighty God and a reverential fear inspires us. Thus it was with John the Baptist who thought himself not worthy to loose the strap of Christ's sandal.[8] So it was with the crowds who heard His words: "And they were astonished by His teaching; for He was teaching them as one having authority, and not as the scribes." [9]

This reaction is even more accentuated in the face of His miracles: it is amazement.[10] Sometimes it is enthusiasm: they recognize Him as the predicted prophet; they wish to make

Him king.[11] Even the possessed are constrained by His power to render Him homage and to prostrate themselves before Him.[12] And there is Peter who, after the miraculous catch of fish, cries: "Depart from me, for I am a sinful man, O Lord." And the evangelist adds: "For he and all who were with him were amazed at the catch of fish they had made."[13] Jesus appeared as living in a world other than that here below, especially when He dealt with the forces of nature—e.g., when He calmed the storm on the lake: "And they feared exceedingly and said to one another, 'Who, then, is This, that even the wind and the sea obey Him?'"[14] The interior mystery of Jesus is clearly manifested at the Transfiguration: Jesus participates in the divine glory.[15]

Even aside from these extraordinary manifestations, the disciples had the feeling that Jesus lived in uncommon intimacy with God; they were so impressed by His solitary prayer, that they asked Him to teach them how to pray.[16] Moreover, a good number of Jesus' sayings reveal His secret life of union with the Father, which sets Him apart from other men. It is the same interior mystery that the soldiers who arrested Him in the Garden of Olives suddenly perceived in His speech and which cast them back on the ground;[17] and the same for the centurion who witnessed the signs accompanying Jesus' last moments on the cross.[18] Finally, after the Resurrection, Jesus' separation from the world is most noticeable. Thenceforth He lives in a spiritual zone from which He seems to come forth at times to appear intermittently among His disciples. His body has assumed qualities which signify belonging to another world.

Jesus makes the group of disciples share in this personal separation. He takes them from their environment by calling them to Himself.[19] They will remain attached to Him by a personal definitive bond; they will "follow" Him and share

His destiny; they must accept the totality of His teaching. The least hesitation raises the decisive question: "Do you also wish to go away?"[20] They are set apart, and their convictions as well as their conduct must be opposed to that of the Pharisees: "Beware of the leaven of the Pharisees."[21] Such separation served to unify the band of disciples and let them enter more intimately into the mystery Jesus was communicating to them: "All things that I have heard from My Father I have made known to you."[22] They will even be so united to Him that it will be necessary to speak of oneness: "And the glory that Thou hast given Me, I have given to them, that they may be one, even as We are one."[23]

After the Ascension, the band of disciples stayed together; they were animated by their own interior life and clearly distinguished from both the pagans and the Jews. It is useless to insist upon this separation here. It would suffice to run through the Acts to recount a mass of facts which show this. These are the beginnings of the Church founded by Christ, mysteriously directed by Him, who is its head, under the inspiration of the Holy Spirit, and who will continue to march at the head of the new Chosen People throughout the centuries.

These aspects then of the Old and New Testament are clear, but we have yet to ask in what exactly this separation consists. As to the Old Testament, there is no great difficulty, for Abraham, his descendants, and then the people of Israel, appear clearly separated from other nations. But when we encounter the teachings of Jesus, we are confronted with a paradox. For the more the disciple realizes he must separate himself from the world, the more he must remain here to conquer it. This is because there are two aspects to this world.

The world from which we must separate is the world in opposition to Christ: "If the world hates you, know that it has hated Me before you. If you were of the world, the world would love what is its own. But because you are not of the world, but I have chosen you out of the world, therefore the world hates you." [24] Jesus has entered into battle with the world by His very mission, and He has triumphed over it: "I have overcome the world." [25] The world can have no part in His intercession: "Not for the world do I pray." [26] In these statements, Jesus is concerned with creatures under the mastery of the forces of evil: "Do not love the world, or the things that are in the world . . . because all that is in the world is the lust of the flesh, and the lust of the eyes, and the pride of life; which is not from the Father, but from the world." [27]

Yet we must remain in the world. But this word has an altogether different meaning in other New Testament passages than it has above. The very Word of God descended into the world: "It was the true light that enlightens every man who comes into the world." [28] It is the object of God's love: "For God so loved the world that He gave His only-begotten Son." [29] And when Jesus departed, He left His disciples here: "And I am no longer in the world, but these are in the world." [30] Jesus died for this world; it is the world He came to save. It is the domain to be conquered, a domain which is to become the kingdom of God.

The paradox disappears when we realize that the primary separation is inside man. Certain Gospel texts suggest this. Thus Jesus' words to the Samaritan woman: "Woman, believe Me, the hour is coming when neither on this mountain nor in Jerusalem will you worship the Father. . . . But the hour is coming, and is now here, when the true worshipers will worship the Father in spirit and in truth. For the Father also seeks such to worship Him." [31] Besides, the food laws concerning cleanness do not protect man, if his heart is already corrupted. "There is nothing outside a man that, entering into him, can defile him; but the things that come out of a man, these are what defile a man. . . . For from within, out of the heart of men, come evil thoughts." [32]

Nevertheless, the exterior separations are an aid to interior detachment. The physical separation and the liberation of the soul form an inseparable unit. This was so even in the Old Testament. It was only in the ages of decadence that the prescriptions of the law became materialistic, to be observed rigorously to the letter. The prophets forcefully recalled the people to fidelity. Thus Osee reproaches Israel for her corruption: "The Lord has a grievance against the inhabitants of the land: there is no fidelity, no mercy." [33] Worship has become purely external: "When Ephraim made many altars to expiate sin, his altars became occasions of sin. Though I write for him my many ordinances, they are considered as a stranger's. Though they offer sacrifice, immolate flesh and eat it, the Lord is not pleased with them." [34] Amos, in the name of Yahweh, said the same thing: "I hate, I spurn your feasts, I take no pleasure in your solemnities; your cereal offerings I will not accept, nor consider your stall-fed peace offerings. But if you would offer Me holocausts, then let justice surge like water, and goodness like an unfailing stream. Did you bring Me sacrifices and offerings for forty years in the desert, O house of Israel?" [35]

Thus, when we say that this separation is first of all within man, we do not mean that the exterior is not important. But exterior objects exercise an influence only inasmuch as man receives them into his heart. They must not dominate or lead. This principle of liberation guides Paul in his Epistles: "All things are lawful for me, but not all things are expedient. All things are lawful for me, but I shall not be brought under the power of anyone." [36] We will be dominated by exterior creatures if we let waves of sensations penetrate us indiscriminately. To be passive in regard to objects is to be led by the impression of the moment. But in this case, it is not the exterior world that gives direction to our activity; it is our own tendencies and their aberrations resulting from sin. Such will not accomplish the task of consecrating the world to God. On the contrary, these complexities contribute to and further accentuate the deformities of the world.

It is necessary, then, to break these interior complexities. This is possible only if we retain control over all the images which come from outside. And such a domination is effective only if the refusal of certain images guarantees freedom in accepting others. This is equivalent to setting limits which prevent certain objects from affecting the feelings and attracting man to them.

In all this, it is not a question of simple personal ascetics to establish the individual in peace (or in *ataraxia*), procuring for him a certain moral equilibrium. The kingdom of God is the goal, and this means restoring the creatures of this world, and man along with them, in Christ. That is what Saint Paul speaks of as freedom in the Lord. The case of the slave is pertinent: "Wast thou a slave when called? Let it not trouble thee. But if thou canst become free, make use of it rather. For a slave who has been called in the Lord, is a freedman of the Lord." [37] The Christian is free because of his baptism. He was plunged into the death of Christ to rise again with Him unto a new life, unto the life of the free children of God. But this life of freedom is not yet perfect. This freedom must grow through a liberation from surrounding creatures. Before this liberation can be accomplished, the Christian must get a perspective with regard to created objects, so that they do not dominate him, but he conquers them and consecrates them to God by progressively integrating them into their fullness in the kingdom.

It follows that this necessary separation from the surrounding world first takes place in the Church. The Church furnishes the Christian the means of protection. For the Church is a living, structured body, and this spiritual armor—yet resting upon the sensible and profoundly woven into it—constitutes a habitual milieu, a foyer where each member of the Church finds strength and defense so he can use the objects of the world and introduce them into the heart of the Church.

From the earliest times, we see this care to set up bulwarks which will serve as a defense and yet not prevent participation in the life of the world. There were divergent tendencies in the early communities: the apostles met to determine what attitude to take henceforth with regard to the Jewish and pagan environment. To maintain circumcision would shackle the Church to Judaism and would hamper the mission to go "teach and baptize all nations." So they commanded the new converts only "to abstain from anything that has been contaminated by idols and from immorality and from anything strangled and from blood." [38]

The protective armor is but the exterior aspect of the community's way of life. Interior was communion with the society of the Three Divine Persons and this communion was maintained principally by gathering for prayer. The first glimpses of the original community are thus characterized: "All these with one mind continued steadfastly in prayer." [39] And when Paul writes to various Christian communities, he counsels them to maintain this environment of piety: ". . . speaking to one another in psalms and hymns and spiritual songs, singing and making melody in your hearts to the Lord, giving thanks always for all things in the name of our Lord Jesus Christ to God the Father." [40]

We see uncertainties and hesitations within the first Christian communities over how strict this separation was to be. There is an echo of this in the Epistles of Saint Paul. Thus many Thessalonians believed that the kingdom founded by

Jesus was approaching its completion: the day of the Lord was imminent. What good is it to mix in the activities of the world? It is useless to work! Paul returns to these points twice, at first discreetly in the First Epistle to the Thessalonians,[41] then quite openly in the Second: "Do not be too hastily shaken from your right mind, nor terrified, whether by spirit, or by utterance, or by letter attributed to us, as though the day of the Lord were near at hand." [42] "For we have heard that some among you are living irregularly, doing no work but busy at meddling. Now such persons we charge and exhort in the Lord Jesus Christ that they work quietly and eat their own bread." [43]

At Corinth, meat sacrificed to idols was the subject of controversy. The more liberal spirits saw no need for rigorous abstention. The idols were nothing; by buying and eating meat that had been offered to them one in no way compromised the sanctity of the body of the Church. But there was a danger of scandalizing certain less enlightened ones. To them this was participation in idolatrous worship. Charity toward them made it necessary to abstain. Thus there was another way to wound the body of Christ and this had to be avoided at all cost: "And through thy 'knowledge' the weak one will perish, the brother for whom Christ died." [44] So the rules of separation should sometime be extended even further to protect the sanctity of the body of the Church and to let her more perfectly conquer the world for Christ: "Therefore, if food scandalizes my brother, I will eat no flesh, no more forever, lest I scandalize my brother." [45]

On this occasion, Saint Paul poses the general principle: we have been freed by Christ, we are free with regard to every creature; nevertheless, the conquest of the world imposes restrictions on this liberty: "For, free though I was as to all, unto all I have made myself a slave that I might gain the more converts." [46]

Practical applications can vary, but the goal remains, and we must not lose sight of it. The Christian, he whom we now call the layman, is deeply committed to the activities of the world; but he must dominate creation, he must be totally detached from it in order to lead it with him into the kingdom of God. Saint Paul explains again regarding marriage: "But this I say, brethren, the time is short; it remains that those who have wives be as if they had none; and those who weep, as though not weeping; and those who rejoice, as though not rejoicing; and those who buy, as though not possessing; and those who use this world, as though not using it, for this world as we see it is passing away." [47]

The variety of solutions results not from differing points of view, as in the case of idol-offerings. An evolution in Christian attitudes toward the world is tied up with different historical situations. It is necessary that the ecclesiastical community be a solidly founded milieu, a hearth truly burning with divine life, the center of a conquering dynamism. On the other hand, if the mission of the Church in the world is to be effective, she must acquire a sort of familiarity with this world. So each time the Church finds herself faced with a new non-Christian environment, she begins by concentrating her forces within herself and the separation becomes more clear. Then, little by little, Christians are allowed to take more of a part in this environment. If they have acquired the interior supports to guard them against all compromise with the surrounding environment, then the work of conquest is realized as Christ commanded, as yeast penetrates and leavens all the dough. [48] At first, the people of God could be formed only in strict separation. In the course of the Church's history, changes occurred. At first, the early Christians kept apart from the pagan environment. They were forbidden to take part in certain professions: the military, the theater, etc. Regarding Islam, and more recently regarding the customs of the Far East or of Africa, the first attitude of the Church has often been one of reserve. Attempts to assimilate the purely human elements came later.

Yet another view determines different degrees of separation. Among Christians, some are more sensitive to the danger of the world's seductions, so they insist on the necessity of separation to safeguard the kingdom of Christ. Many among these decided, especially after the Peace of Constantine, to attain an absolute separation by retiring to the desert. We must add that this movement was providential in procuring an important bulwark for the spiritual life of the Church. In time, cenobite communities were set up which sought to realize a perfect image of the kingdom of God, completely separate from the world. Other Christians, widows, virgins, or celibates, led a life of separation while living within the ecclesiastical community. Sometimes they devoted themselves to works of charity, either for the poor or for the sick.

Often these departures from the world were occasioned by historic circumstances. Thus the great movement to the desert began with the Edict of Constantine at the beginning of the fourth century. From then on it would no longer be possible to join the Lord by martyrdom; the solitary life with its total detachment from material things and with its union with the Lord in perpetual prayer would be a substitute. Yet, the choice of this form of life is based on the word of Christ.

This is the road marked by Jesus in the episode of the rich young man.[49] He was dealing there, first of all with the destiny of every man: each must strive for eternal life. This is the fundamental question: "Good Master, what shall I do to gain eternal life?"[50] That there are two roads to travel here is the meaning of Jesus' reply. One may remain involved in the affairs of the world; this is legitimate, this can even be good. But then, in these affairs, it is necessary to use the right means, observing each of the commandments. These keep one from using creatures proudly and selfishly. At the same time, they prescribe the way of leading all to their true natural end, and ultimately to God. If during his youth the rich man had already observed all this faithfully, perhaps it was because of a hidden desire in the depths of his soul, a secret call to approach God by a more simple life, that very one which Christ revealed to him: "If thou wilt be perfect, go, sell what thou hast, and give to the poor, and thou shalt have treasure in heaven; and come follow Me." [51] But he refused this total giving: "But when the young man heard the saying, he went away sad, for he had great possessions." [52]

The same question can be asked regarding marriage and the use of human affections. Following a discussion with the Pharisees concerning divorce, the disciples commented: "If the case of a man with his wife is so, it is not expedient to marry." And Jesus responds: "Not all can accept this teaching; but those to whom it has been given. For there are eunuchs who were born so from their mother's womb; and there are eunuchs who were made so by men; and there are eunuchs who have made themselves so for the sake of the kingdom of heaven. Let him accept it who can." [53]

If not all hear, doubtless it is because some do not want to hear. But it is also true that the call to live totally separated from the world is not addressed to all. Thus two roads are indicated, both of which embrace the task of consecrating the world to God. It is important to consider what differentiates them.

What we have seen up to now clearly shows that separation is not the differentiating factor. Every Christian is one set apart. His citizenship is already "in heaven." [54] He has been "rescued from the power of darkness and transferred into the kingdom of the beloved Son." [55] He can fulfill his task only if he maintains this state of separation.

Neither does the distinction lie in the external and internal separation: the monk or the religious being isolated from the world by an exterior barrier, the layman keeping his distance only by spiritual means.

First, as we have already noted, the sensible means and the desire for separation must be a unit. But especially if one takes a bird's-eye view of religious history, he sees that the degree of interiorization of the separation depends upon the tasks assumed by the religious. At first, a complete armor placed the religious in a world apart. But certain religious orders received a vocation which called them to work in the world. For this they needed more flexibility of action, and many external practices had to be abandoned. In compensation, the spiritual structures had to be all the more solid. The Society of Jesus abandoned the choral office, but gave capital importance to methodical prayer. Conversely, for a long time, our laymen copied the organization of their spiritual life from the daily life of monasteries. Only later, in view of the needs arising from a more exacting apostolic commitment, did a new view develop. Yet one sees identical tasks assumed both by laymen, and by religious or clerics.

We must take into account that, if all Christians tend toward God, their sovereign Good, they do not arrive at perfection immediately, but through earthly and sensible goods. However, let us distinguish, in the first place, man in the common situation. He prepares here below for eternal life by living in a sort of city which anticipates the heavenly city and which offers him an environment in which his personality can develop. What does this mean? He finds in the midst of the earthly city the possibility of concentrating all his good tendencies toward a single purpose in this earthly city, and this purpose is a means to the ultimate goal. For example, all the activities of the artist are crystallized in the goal of art, taking up all his concrete human life: family, professional, social, etc. All, so to say, contribute to this superior activity; but this itself finds a place in the earthly city as one of its dynamic elements. At least this would be the ideal. If he is Christian, the layman, through this intermediate end, aims at the final end which is God, by living in a certain union with Him here below. He already finds an expansion of his personality on this natural level; this natural life is, as it were, an image of the supernatural life. And this is true for all human vocations which are capable of expanding personality.

The religious, for his part, can also assume human activities; but he integrates them directly into the kingdom of God, of which his community is a concretization. One and the other, layman and religious, taking part in terrestrial activities must in a way be separated from them by grace of a certain detachment, lest they renounce the dominion they must exercise over these things. But, beyond this, the religious separates functionally from the world in that he cannot establish himself in the world, even provisionally. By his vows he is already established, so to speak, in the eschatological goal. He has placed his will completely in the hands of God. The layman, for his part, is established in the earthly city, but in view of the heavenly one.

The separation of the layman engaged in the world constitutes a negative aspect of his vocation. He must positively consecrate the world to God. This is beyond his own power. He can do it only in Christ. This opens up even more perspectives on the spirituality of laymen.

FOOTNOTES:

[1] Gn. 12, 1.

[2] Gn. 18, 23–33.

[3] Gn. 32, 29.

[4] Gn. 45, 5–8.

[5] Ex. 16, 3; 17, 3; Nm. 20, 2ff; Ex. 16, 2; Nm. 11, 4ff.

[6] Ex. 19, 5–6.

[7] Os. 2, 16.

[8] Jn. 1, 27.

[9] Mk. 1, 22.

[10] Mk. 1, 27; cf. Lk. 9, 43; 11, 14; Mt. 9, 23.

[11] Jn. 6, 14; cf. Mk. 7, 37.

[12] Mk. 3, 11; cf. Mk. 5, 6.

[13] Lk. 5, 8–9.

[14] Mk. 4, 41; cf. 6, 5.

[15] Mk. 9, 2ff and parallel passages.

[16] Lk. 11, 1.

[17] Jn. 18, 6.

[18] Mk. 15, 39.

[19] Mk. 1, 17–20; Jn. 1, 38–50.

[20] Jn. 6, 68.

[21] Mk. 8, 15.

[22] Jn. 15, 15.

[23] Jn. 17, 22.

[24] Jn. 15, 18–19.

[25] Jn. 16, 33.

[26] Jn. 17, 9.

[27] 1 Jn. 2, 15–16.

[28] Jn. 1, 9.

[29] Jn. 3, 16.

[30] Jn. 17, 11.

[31] Jn. 4, 21.23.

[32] Mk. 7, 15.21.

[33] Os. 4, 1.

[34] Os. 8, 11–14.

[35] Am. 5, 21–25.
[36] 1 Cor. 6, 12.
[37] 1 Cor. 7, 21–22.
[38] Acts 15, 20.
[39] Acts 1, 14; cf. 4, 24–30.
[40] Eph. 5, 19–20; cf. Col. 3, 16.
[41] 1 Thes. 4, 11; 5, 1–2.
[42] 2 Thes. 2, 2.
[43] 2 Thes. 3, 11–12.
[44] 1 Cor. 8, 11.
[45] 1 Cor. 8, 13.
[46] 1 Cor. 9, 19.
[47] 1 Cor. 7, 29–31.
[48] Cf. Mt. 13, 33.
[49] Cf. Mk. 10, 17–27.
[50] Mk. 10, 17.
[51] Mt. 19, 21.
[52] Mt. 19, 22.
[53] Mt. 19, 10–12.
[54] Phil. 3, 20.
[55] Col. 1, 31.

4

The Sacrifice of Christ, Center
of the Consecration of the World

The Christian's vocation is to attain God, to lead the created world into His mystery. This is impossible without the religious structures which form the foundations of the city of God. From these the Christian gets the strength he needs to leaven the profane world and yet not be seduced by it.

This task then is not merely human. It is realized in the midst of a truly human life, but it far surpasses human capabilities. It involves, in effect, rediscovering full participation in divine life. So God Himself had to take the initiative. He sent His Son into the world to lay hold of this created world in the depths of its being and again integrate it into the life of the Trinity. Since man is the focal point of all the creatures in the world, the Son became flesh, assumed a *human* nature: "And the Word was made flesh." [1] Jesus came as head of humanity and thus of all creation. Because He was the Second Person of the Trinity and had this unique hold on creation He had the power to gather all things together in the heart of the Divinity: "He is the image of the invisible God, the firstborn of every creature. For in Him were created all things." [2]

In fact, His life establishes a road along which He draws

men, and all creatures with them, into the kingdom. Its summit is the redemptive act of the sacrifice of the cross. At that moment, He rescued man from the depths of the abyss of death, "the wages of sin," [3] a necessary result of separation from God, to implant in him the most perfect act of love, to reestablish all in the love of God. Everything focuses on this "hour" when Jesus "passes out of this world to the Father"; [4] all is sealed in this instant, "it is consummated." [5] That which the crossing of the Red Sea and the passage from slavery in Egypt to freedom in the Promised Land long ago prefigured, Jesus fulfilled in reality, by passing from death to life, and by granting that every man who would believe in Him be plunged into His death to rise again to eternal life.

The Passion, the Cross, and the Resurrection, completed in the Ascension, constitute a single redemptive act which draws upon all the sentiments, all the acts, and all the intentions of Christ's life. Throughout His life, Jesus, in the depths of His soul, directs all toward the supreme offering. In a unique and final instant, He gathers up all this past life, and in the perfect acceptance of death, He makes the supreme sacrifice which includes all that was begun during His life on earth. This act of obedience and offering effected a turning toward God; there was at this same instant an explosive outpouring in the world of the almighty love of God, an outpouring which reestablished all things. The Resurrection manifested this result.

Because Christ is the head of the humanity He came to renew, His life is also the perfect form for all human existence. And this term *form* must be understood in the strict sense, with a meaning analogous to that which it has in the expression "the soul is the form of the body." Every man who has "put on Christ" in Baptism feels an impulse. An interior dynamism influences his activities, without violating his liberty, to direct them in a new mode of acting conformable to that of Christ.

This is the case, for example, in prayer. One can ask with Saint Thomas why Jesus prayed. He had no need of prayer. The answer is enlightening for our purpose and it is important that we understand it. Saint Thomas answers with the words of Saint Ambrose: "Do not misunderstand what you hear so that you think the Son of God, as if out of weakness, asked to receive what He Himself was not able to fulfill, for He, the author of power and master of obedience, by His example inspired us to follow the precepts of virtue." [6]

The same goes for all the actions and interior sentiments of Christ: all have exemplary value. Not that everyone should repeat His acts, His thoughts, His desires; what is meant here is a participation in an interior dynamism which tends to form men so that they act in union with Jesus according to perfection and the good.

Again, all Christ's actions focus on the supreme act of His sacrifice and receive their value from it. Indeed, the sacrificial act of the cross contains the form of all the acts of His life, and the Christian must put on this form to accomplish in his turn his own acts in union with the sacrifice of Christ. Thus each one must let Christ lead him along the road Saint Paul essentially outlined for the Philippians: "Have this mind in you which also was in Christ Jesus." [7] Then follows the impressive sketch of the mystery of Christ from His divine nature to His obedient descent into the curse of death on a cross and His Resurrection unto glorification.

However, the mystery of the Redemption does not remain in past history. It becomes a present invitation, an attraction, as an immediate possibility interwoven in the life of each man. On Calvary, the redemptive act was accomplished with such perfection as to become a model or rather a "type" capable of attracting all men and transforming them in union with Christ. But on Calvary, this possibility was not presented in a practical way. That was done at the Cenacle. The redemptive act is re-presented by the rite. The sensible symbols of bread and wine are rendered significant and efficacious by Christ's words. In this instant, Jesus' own sacrificial act to the Father, including all its relationships with the circumstances of His life and especially with the sufferings endured in the Passion, are all given to men that their whole personal lives may enter into this mystery. And by the power of Christ, who gave the Apostles the command and power to accomplish this same rite—"Do this in commemoration of me"—the re-presentation of the redemptive act is repeated throughout all times and all lands.

The Cenacle and the Mass thus became the instruments of the New Covenant. By using this Old Testament term, Jesus manifests that this is the fulfillment of what had been already begun. It recalls the covenant which Yahweh sealed with the patriarchs Noe and Abraham, and the people of Israel. This term had been taken from customs widespread at that time. Covenants of power and goods for mutual aid were common. They were often made among equals: peace treaties,[8] agreements among brothers,[9] pacts of friendship.[10] Often too the powerful promised their protection on condition that the protected serve them in return.[11] This relationship with God is, to some extent, analogous. However, it is not just temporal goods which are involved, but the mystery of God also constantly stands in the background. The mystery surrounding this covenant is underlined in the account of Genesis: Abraham, during the night of the alliance, is seized with "terror."[12] On Sinai, God multiplies most impressive manifestations of His power. The effects of this alliance will consist not only in a legal agreement, but in a sort of interpenetration of divine life and human life, to such a point that the glory of God will become the business of man. This is clear on the occasion of Abraham's intercession in favor of the just in Sodom[13] and throughout the sojourn of Israel in the desert. "God desires to lead men to a life of communion with Him. It is this idea, so fundamental to the doctrine of salvation, that the theme of the covenant expresses." [14]

The same goes for the New Covenant. In instituting the Eucharist, Christ put at the disposal of men an instrument for participation in the alliance and thus entry into the intimacy of the Trinity by sharing in the sacrifice of Christ. Clearly Jesus intended to give the rite this meaning. The mention of the covenant is found in all four accounts of the institution. Saint Paul reports the words thus: "This cup is the new covenant in My blood; do this as often as you drink it, in remembrance of Me." [15] The consecration of the bread is also clear; both in Luke and in the First Epistle to the Corinthians these words are used: "My body which is being given for you," [16] "My body which shall be given up for you." [17] That is to say that the sacrifice offered under the efficacious sign of bread and wine is placed at your disposal, that it may freely become your offering, assimilating your own offering. The redemptive act eternalized in glory is re-presented by the Church wherever her members are united in communities. Christ is the unique mediator: the mediation of the Church is not added to that of Christ, but renders the unique mediation of Christ available now for each one.

To render the sacrifice of Christ present, a special consecration is required which configures one to Christ more completely than does Baptism. This consecration is conferred by the sacrament of Orders which confers the priestly character. Thanks to the priest, Christ's sacrifice remains here below constantly. In the Eucharist He acts effectively in all times and in all places.

The layman too is rendered capable of participating in this sacrifice. He is configured to Christ-the-priest by the character of Baptism which Confirmation brings to fullness in him. The human nature of Christ with all the powers of His soul, intellect, will, and feelings, in being assumed by the person of the Son, received a consecration rendering it able to be the divinity's perfect instrument for bringing all creation to God through the sacrifice of the cross. Because the Christian is a member of Christ, he participates in this action; that is, he bears within himself, so to say, all creatures existing in his time and in his environment. On the cross, Christ extended His hands, giving us to understand that He would embrace the universe. Christians become like the hands of Christ which effectively lay hold of these beings which the Lord has already attracted, to plunge them into the intimacy of the Trinity. The priest is at the hearth of this mystery of love, and the layman stands at the door to bring in first himself and then, with him, the rest of creation. Thus every baptized person, by the character of this sacrament, shares in the priesthood of Christ and receives the capacity to be freely drawn into the eucharistic mystery of Christ acting now.

There are two aspects to this participation. The baptized has the power to enter into Christ's mystery under the leadership of the priest; he offers creation through, with and in Christ for consecration to God. He also receives grace and power to prepare for this consecration by acting as the Lord's instrument introducing into the heart of the world a preparatory degree of sanctity. These two functions are inseparable: participation in the eucharistic mystery could not be authentic if it were not related to the human task in the world, and it could have no eternal value if it were not vivified by the graces issuing from the sacrifice of Christ. Both functions are free. That is why man is responsible for the salvation of the entire world. Let us consider separately these two functions proper to the layman, functions which are the basis of his spirituality.

Participation in Christ's sacrifice is essential to the Christian's life. His vocation here below is to enter more and more into the kingdom of heaven, constantly to make more perfect his belonging to God, and to aid all those creatures in any way dependent upon him to attain this same end. The Mass, as the re-presentation of this sacrifice, is the instrument *par excellence* for progress and growth in the Christian's life. At Mass, Christ is present offering His sacrifice and applying its fruits to all those who would unite in it. He is "the door of the sheep." "I am the door," Jesus said. "If anyone enter by Me he shall be safe, and shall go in and out and shall find pastures." [18] Even when the Christian is capable of any other action, if he unites himself as perfectly as he can with Christ's sacrifice offered at Mass, he accomplishes the greatest possible act, he raises the world.

Thus the Mass must be the center of the layman's life. Even if the time he spends at Mass is short relative to the length of his life, his most profound intention, which gives value to his actions and establishes an order of preference among them, must place the Mass at the summit of his life. To obtain this he has only to make the Church's intention his own: Sunday, the day on which we celebrate the mystery of the Lord is the first day of the week. Not only according to an ordinal understanding which ranks it as the first of a series of days, but also ontologically: this mystery diffuses its rays and exercises an attraction on all the other days, giving them a value of sanctity. Further, the eucharistic mystery is renewed each day, as far as possible, to vivify with supernatural life the elementary rhythm of time, the alternation of days and nights.

To participate most effectively in the Mass, it is important for the layman to understand well the dispositions with which he should take part. From beginning to end, the Mass is presented as an invitation addressed to the faithful to enter into the mystery. The Mass does not consist of a succession of roles which each takes in his turn—the role of priest representing the Church, the role of the people representing the laity, and then the role of Christ. All act constantly, but each in his own way according to his own station. Above all, Christ does not cease to offer. The sacrifice of Christ does not succeed a sacrifice of the Church, substituting for it while identified with it. The whole action is one unique sacrifice, that of Christ which encompasses that of the Church, that of the priest, and that of the laity. It is offered by Christ, by the Church, by the priest, and by the faithful, but in different ways. The sacrifice of Christ reaches its culmination in the consecration; nevertheless, it starts at the beginning of the Mass and continues all the way to its finish. And throughout the Mass, Christ, the Church, the priest, and the faithful do not cease to act.

Thus the readings bring Christ's light to demonstrate and accomplish the work of redemption; at the same time it is the Church which spreads this word to her entire body in the present time; the priest gives it to the community for whom he celebrates *hic et nunc;* finally, each of the faithful receives it and makes it his own to enlighten his daily task and to prepare the creatures of the world to enter in their turn into the mystery of the Lord.

Also the prayers of supplication are Christ's who intercedes unceasingly for us, but at the same time these prayers belong to the Church which prays with Him, since they are the prayers of Christ Himself praying in the Church which is His body. The priest, representing the hierarchy of the Church, makes the prayer present for the Christian people in this place. Finally, the faithful place these requests on their lips and make them their own. Yet all the while, these words remain the meritorious and infallible prayer of Christ, in the measure in which each one adheres personally to Him by faith.

The offering expressed in the course of the offertory has for materials the bread and wine. But here they are not just the common food of man, they are gifts *for* Christ's sacrifice. It is Christ then who offers. But at the same time, He accepts the offering of the whole Church. The priest is the instrument of this intention of the Lord. Finally, the layman must become receptive to this intention; then his own free act of offering is also stirred in the depths of his heart. The more receptive he is to the mysterious intention of Christ, the more his entire life, including all his earthly attachments, is incorporated into the sacrifice of Christ.

The sacrifice of Christ is then woven throughout the Mass in His body, the Church, and consequently in each member of this body, the laymen. The human instrument of this action is the priest; but everyone is active in responding to this action offered for his free acceptance. This takes place in the unfolding of a celebration, for it requires a weaving into human life whose very tissue is, so to say, duration. Therefore the slowness of the liturgical celebration should be considered relative to the time required for the divine mystery to penetrate all the powers of man: intelligence which it enlightens by faith, the feelings which it arouses, and finally the will which consents.

It is like a climb which culminates in the supreme instant of the consecration in which the essentials of the redemptive act are made present, and in which at the same time the participants are vested with the risen Christ, progressing into the heart of the mystery to the degree that their wills are opened to the love of Christ.

From this summit graces flow into the concrete human life opened by the reception of Communion. It is always Christ who acts to take possession of the portion of the world upon which the redemptive grace has been called; it is He who stirs up in the Church this new force of apostolic conquest and who multiplies it in the heart of each of the faithful. At the same time, there mounts to the Lord a homage of adoration and thanksgiving, itself stirred up by Christ in His Church. This sense is found in its fullness in this hymn of the Apocalypse: "Worthy art Thou, O Lord our God, to receive glory and honor and power; for Thou hast created all things, and because of Thy will they existed, and were created." [19]

There is a continuity and interpenetration between the action of Christ, that of the Church, and that of the members. Nevertheless, these diverse actions and participations are underlined by their respective roles during the celebration. The different aspects of the reality can be expressed in human language only successively. So the texts and rites are different. Even if, in their human consciousness, the participants may not always clearly perceive the diverse aspects of the reality, they are nonetheless there. As to the redemptive act of Christ, there is no difficulty in seeing its continuity. As to the human participation, it is maintained by the persistence of the intention. If the will is entrusted to that of Christ by a free act, so long as that will is not retracted the functional attitude remains always the same, orientated as it must be for all human acts.

If Christ's redemptive act is made present and at the same time rouses in the participants a free reception, a personal response, one can see the importance of dialogue in the liturgy. This receptiveness should persevere throughout the celebration. But, we should note, it is necessary from time to time that the consciousness be called to attention. The responses which the assembly makes, the common chants in which they participate, keep them constantly alert. The faithful understood this better perhaps in early Christianity. For example: "At the end of the eucharistic prayer, when the consecrated gifts lay upon the altar, when the offering to the Divine Majesty had been expressed and the mighty prayer brought to its conclusions with *Per ipsum et cum ipso et in ipso,* the entire community voiced its assent in the *Amen.* Saint Jerome recounts how, in the Roman basilicas, this *Amen* used to resound like a thunder-clap." [20]

Dialogue is not simply the alternation of words. It is a way of reciprocal penetration into the consciousness of one another and aims toward an agreement of mind and will. Since one of the speakers is God, obviously the aim is a perfect con-formity to His will. Throughout the Mass, the dialogue neces-sarily bears on the sacrifice of Christ. It stimulates the partici-pants to enter into the mystery of immolation and offering. It brings them by leading them personally and all that belongs to them into the offering, and vests their own gifts with the perfect gift of Christ.

Actions are joined with the words to express a real commit-ment. Even though in the course of time they have been at-tenuated, they nevertheless continue to evoke more extensive rites and preserve their full significance. Thus the modest gesture of making one's contribution at the offertory recalls the solemn collection of the offerings of the faithful in an offertory procession. In addition, the blessing at the end of the canon recalls the goods of the earth which receive a share in the graces brought by the sacrifice of Christ. But already the priest has pronounced over the offerings placed on the altar these words which accompany the blessings: "Through Him (Christ), Lord (God), You ever create all these good things, sanctify, vivify, bless, and give them to us. *Per quem haec omnia, Domine, semper bona creas, sanctificas, vivificas, benedicis, et praestas nobis."* [21]

We now come to the second function of the layman in the

consecration of the world: his involvement in a human task through which he sees to the penetration into creatures of the graces issuing from Christ's sacrifice, graces destined to render these creatures holy. In effect, every Christian is sent into the world by Christ. We spoke, in the second chapter, of man's conquest of the world. This is the task God has entrusted to him from the beginning of time. The Christian, like every other man, has to accomplish this. But it would be an error to dissociate human activity, transforming the world by labor, from the redemptive act. One cannot, as is sometimes done, oppose the work of the layman in the world to the vocation of the religious, as if the order of creation were reserved to the former and that of redemption to the latter. The Christian in the world continues to improve the conditions of life on earth; he seeks to bring more peace and happiness. But his activity is at the same time spiritualizing to a high degree. We repeat: for the Christian the human vocation is transfigured. Every time he deals with creatures in the world—whether it is a question of himself or the beings around him—to understand and transform them, he draws them more and more from the profane world, bringing them further into the kingdom of God; he directs them more and more toward their final goal, he sows in the hearts of these beings a stronger and stronger attraction to God, their Master and their Father. And he draws this power from Christ's sacrifice, that is from the redemptive act of Christ made present by the sacrifice of the Mass, made ready for application to these creatures *hic et nunc* for their continual consecration to God.

The efficacy of the Christian's action in the world is conditioned by his situation in its midst. He is not in the world as an isolated individual. His life is linked with it; the world belongs to him, it is the extension of his being. These bonds which link surrounding creatures to man are natural and realize the will of God clearly expressed in the revelation at the beginning of Genesis. We have already touched on this in chapter two. It is important, however, to stress it here, because the spirituality of laymen must be based on these natural relations.

First, the being which belongs to each man is not limited to his body. Man somehow extends his being as far as his senses reach. And the instruments which multiply the power of the senses enlarge still more his personal frontiers. Take a simple stick which allows one to touch an object beyond the reach of his hand. The end of the stick carries the tactile sense: *I* touch something with the tip of my cane. We can say that even the most perfect machines are, in a way, only extensions of our senses since the technically constructed mechanisms participate in the physiological apparatus of the reflex. The movements of machines are accomplished with mechanisms similar to those of the living body.

Indeed, man spontaneously utilizes his experience to construct the exterior world about himself as its center. The exploration accomplished by the child, in as much as it awakens his consciousness and expands his powers, is not like a simple intrusion among objects from which he gains nothing. They are put in relation to each other and finally joined to self. They are like trail signs one comes across in the heart of a thick forest which allow rediscovery of the way. We know how, as one passes from object to object, they are colored by a certain familiarity, the feeling of having already seen them. An instinctive function never ceases to act and continually perfects this organization and points out by degrees a sort of plan in the surrounding world.

I know, for example, that this room in which I am working opens on a hall and is part of first an apartment, and then a building in which I can move about in reality or in imagination without getting lost. This house is not isolated, but rests solidly on the ground and is part of a city—and so on, since the totality of my environment is consistent. As my experience progresses, the interior organization perfects itself and includes the new objects.

It sometimes happens that one keenly realizes this function of organization. Thus it is with the memories of childhood. A departure for a vacation leaves the child with the impression of a transfer into a dream world which the child records as distasteful to his habitual environment. The experience of Proust, with regard to the madeleine dunked in tea, also betrays this constructive self-activity. If it could construct a memory like this rising from a special sensation of joy, it is, without doubt, because it functions habitually: "When I recognized the taste of the morsel of madeleine soaked in the lime-blossom tea which my aunt gave me . . . the old gray house on the street, where her room was, changed. It was as if the decor of a theater had come to cover the little pavilion opening onto the garden. I had built it for my parents in their last years . . . and along with the house, the city too changed from morning to night and all the time, the place where they sent me before lunch, the streets where I went to run, the paths we took if the weather was good. And as in that game in which the Japanese amuse themselves by dunking indistinct pieces of paper into a porcelain bowl, which pieces, when plunged in, stretch out, take on shape and color and specific features and become flowers, houses, formed and recognizable people, in this same way now all the flowers of our garden and those of Mr. Swann's part, the water lilies of the Vivonne, the good people of the village, their little dwellings and the Church, all Combray and its environs, all these took solid form and came out, city and gardens, from my cup of tea." [22]

There is also a counter-proof of the existence of this function.

In certain pathological cases the subject complains, though all the while in his own room, of feeling lost. He no longer knows where this room is situated, nor where the house is located in relation to the rest of the world. This function of relation is disturbed.

The world in which we live is not made up of things only, but, even more, of human beings. In this too, relationships are born and set up social structures in which men find themselves bound one to another. On the elementary level, we need only mention the awareness of the presence of others, which has such an influence on one's attitude, gestures, and manner of expression. The image of the person as one sees it results in a variation of reactions. One does not act in the presence of a child nor in the presence of an influential person as if one were alone. As Pierre Janet would have said, a higher degree of psychic tension is needed to read the same text before the public than to read it in private.

Other relationships arise when one has to be in charge of someone—a subordinate or a dependent—or even when he must simply deal *with* another. Each of these cases would have to be analyzed in its own complexity; it suffices here to have pointed out a line of investigation.

Finally, the highest degree of action among men is that which involves a reciprocity of relations. One gives himself to others in order to accomplish a common objective, and this he does in a relationship of simple friendship or love. Yet this supposes an agreement in which each adapts himself to the other more and more perfectly by a disinterested giving of self which transcends both persons.

Thus arises about each person throughout the world of things and men a network of extremely complex relationships. These are the relationships which must finally be rejoined to God in and through Christ. But one realizes that this last bond cannot be sealed unless the relationships in the world are already in harmony with those of the kingdom of God into which Christ introduces us. An important task of realignment and achievement is offered to the Christian in the world. This we shall examine in the following chapter.

FOOTNOTES:

[1] Jn. 1, 14.

[2] Col. 1, 15–16.

[3] Rom. 6, 23.

[4] Jn. 13, 1.

[5] Jn. 19, 30.

[6] *Summa Theologiae,* III, q. 21, a. 1, I^m: *"Noli insidiatrices aperire aures, ut putes Filium Dei quasi infirmum rogare, ut impetret quod implere non possit, potestatis enim auctor, obedientiae magister, ad praecepta virtutis suo nos informat exemplo."*

[7] Phil. 2, 5.

[8] Gn. 14, 13; 21, 22ff, etc.

[9] Am. 1, 9.

[10] 1 Sm. 23, 58.

[11] Cf. Jos. 9, 11–15; 1 Sm. 11, 1; 2 Sm. 3, 12ff.

[12] Gn. 15, 12.

[13] Gn. 18, 22–33.

[14] X. Léon-Dufour, *Vocabulaire de théologie biblique,* Paris, 1962, col. 20.

[15] 1 Cor. 11, 25.

[16] Lk. 22, 19.

[17] 1 Cor. 11, 24.

[18] Jn. 10, 7.9.

[19] Ap. 4, 11.

[20] J. A. Jungmann, *The Sacrifice of the Church, the Meaning of the Mass,* Collegeville, Minn.: Liturgical Press, 1956, p. 33.

[21] Prayers of the canon of the Mass before the minor elevation.

[22] Marcel Proust, *Du côté de chez Swann,* Vol. I, p. 49.

5

The Sacraments, Instruments
of the Consecration of the World

The cross of Christ is hereafter at the center of the world as the sign of salvation. Calvary opens the floodgates to the flow of divine life. Jesus Christ, leader or head of the new humanity, is filled with grace. From Him grace floods the entire world throughout all time. This salutary inundation filters through the soil of the world, soaking it with divine life. Since the death and resurrection of Christ, the world is in continual travail of childbirth; its divinization progresses ceaselessly until the end of time, when the world will be totally transformed into the kingdom of God, prepared to be offered through Christ, its head, to the eternal Father in the act of final homage.

Where does this divine life, first received in Christ, the new Adam and head of the Mystical Body, enter the world? It enters through each of Jesus' faithful, the members of His body. Each, in fact, receives from the plenitude of grace which Jesus possesses at the center of the world. Each of the faithful becomes a participant in the divine nature. This means that God in Christ is constantly giving him a new degree of being. But this earthly kingdom, which man is to make a harmonious city, is not concerned only with that natural existence which

God constantly maintains by never ceasing to think of each creature and to love it. It includes participation in the intimate being of God which confers on man the divine modes and makes him capable of introducing these into the world.

By this expression "divine modes" we wish to explain the term supernatural *habitus* which the theologian uses to define grace. Imagine a stranger arriving in a far-off country, a European for example in the Far East. He decides to become one of these people among whom he is living. He becomes accustomed little by little to his new fatherland, he learns the language perfectly, he adopts all the customs, he so identifies himself with this world he has entered that we can no longer tell him from a native. However, in the natives' eyes, confusion will be impossible: in the minutest details, in reactions of which the subject himself is unconscious, the stranger will reveal his true origin. Though he has perhaps acquired many of the characteristics of the people, he cannot gain the sort of interior dynamism to unify and command all his reactions, including the less conscious. Let him marry a woman of this country; then his children will receive this capacity proper to their race.

In a way, the same is true of the grace conferred on man. He is "no longer a stranger and foreigner, but a citizen with the saints and a member of God's household." [1] His nature is elevated; it is, so to speak, accommodated to the influx of the Holy Spirit who in a permanent way stirs up in him the flow of divine life which makes him love as God loves and know as God knows in the heart of the Trinity. This capacity is woven into his nature, to the very *depth* of which a Tauler speaks, that is, to the very roots of his being. Though stirred by God, it belongs to the person, it is his own because of his own completely free act which is a complete expression of himself.

Thus we must see that the Christian participates in the divine nature. This means that he himself personally acts with this divine capacity by means of this principle of divine actions continually activated in him by the Holy Spirit. In other words, he really disposes of divine goods as a "joint heir with Christ." [2] Is this not the mysterious reality that suggested this term to Saint Paul?

But, let us repeat, this participation has its roots deep in human nature, beyond the consciousness, in that most secret region where God acts. Listen again to Saint Paul: "The Spirit Himself gives testimony to our spirit that we are sons of God." [3] Man cannot know this directly. The spirit is beyond his grasp. In the far-off country we imagined above, who is able to recognize the authentic native, the citizen belonging to his own race? Only the native himself. So also, who knows when a man lives the life of God but God alone? God alone knows His own nature.

Had there been no sin in the world, this divine life would have developed and permeated all the activities of man and thus all creatures from the very instant of their coming into existence. It would have first stirred up charity, giving a divine quality to the other virtues. Creation itself would have served as the support for mounting continually and harmoniously toward the plenitude of divine life, something like Plato conceived the progressive ascension toward the Good in the seventh book of *The Republic*. The sacraments would probably not have existed; the mutual reaction or aid of creatures would have sufficed. As in the present state of humanity, "in Adam all die," [4] all, in the state of innocence, would have participated in life through the human nature received from Adam.

Now all relive in Christ, the new Adam, but progressively through an application of the redemptive merits of Christ to the diverse circumstances of human life as it is now. The sacraments are the means of this application. Thus they seem principally a remedy for sin, a help allowing man to realize his vocation to consecrate himself and the world with him to God. Thus are the sacraments placed along the path of man's life. They are placed at the critical phases of this life: first at its beginning and, as well, at those moments when it is necessary for a man, by a free act, to cross a new threshold in his ascent to God, to assume freely a new role, and finally to integrate that role in the kingdom. For this he needs a special gift of God.

The first of these roles is that of the man plunged by Baptism into the death of Christ to rise to the new life. The newly baptized begins his pilgrimage toward the heavenly Jerusalem. He is from now on *in Christ,* he has put on Christ, he is enveloped by Him who is the Alpha and the Omega, the beginning and the end. That is to say he is built upon Christ who stirs up this new life in him, and he looks toward Christ as to "Him who comes" and he is drawn by Christ as his goal.

It is evident that Baptism is indispensable not only for conferring the character which makes one capable of offering the sacrifice of Christ, as we have explained above, but also to elevate to God and stir up again the first flow of divine life which will flood all the human life.

It would seem that the neophyte received at Baptism all the equipment necessary to accomplish his earthly sojourn with Christ. But we must not forget that this sacrament does not reestablish man in the state of innocence. The harmonious ascent to God which we described above is no longer possible. Sin entered the world. Christ's act of reparation did not simply annul the evil. It integrated it also as an occasion for even greater good. This is indeed a new circumstance in which man must face the menace of evil. The other sacraments derive their proper roles from this fact.

Baptism created man's essential role in Christ, but it did not immediately mature him from the spiritual point of view. So there are two aspects of Christian life which are related to two sacraments. Baptism constitutes one a child of God, a participant in the entire life of the Church. It confers the essentials that make him capable of interior holiness and of sanctifying his environment, the exterior world to which he is related.

But life in the Church is a life of battle. The forces of evil are at work on all levels. At the basis of this are the evil spirits, the fallen angels, who in spite of their fall have not lost those first relations with the world which God willed according to His design of love. The activities of the demons strengthen the simple tendencies to evil found in man wounded by sin; finally they join with creatures deprived of reason to accentuate the evil seduction these retain because of the primitive destruction of the world's harmony.

But, all these evil forces, each taken in itself, have a true goodness; their malice comes from the fact that they are out of place, that they are directed to a partial end, and that they are turned from God. The task God has given to the man who lives in Him is to take on courageously all these activities and lead them to their true end. Only one who has reached maturity in Christ is capable of this work. The sacrament of Confirmation confers this maturity. Man, in the course of his development, acquires what is called personality, that is, he gains a status in which he takes possession of all his powers and directs them on his own responsibility. In this same way the Christian, by the sacrament of Confirmation, receives the capacity to assume personally all the created powers with which he comes into contact, to lead them to work harmoniously in the body of the Church. He receives a unique personal role in this living body, whence he personally assumes responsibility for the entire Church. He has become a "perfect Christian," as the catechism says, a *mature man,*[5] or that *spiritual man* who "judges all things, and he himself is judged by no man," [6] because he lets himself be guided by the Spirit who has by Confirmation taken possession of him in a new manner.[7]

We can see, then, why there has been an inclination to link together in some way Catholic Action and Confirmation, for truly Catholic Action is aimed at the conquest of every milieu for Christ. Nevertheless, this is only a partial view of things, and the sacrament of Confirmation confers spiritual maturity on each Christian, whatever his age, whether or not he is engaged in an organized action.

Again, spiritual maturity is never complete here below. So let us speak of the capacity conferred by Confirmation. It frequently happens that the Christian falls before the seductions of the world. The Spirit certainly leads, but with a gentleness that excludes all constraint. The appeal of the Spirit is sometimes drowned out by the noises of the world. It can even happen that the faithful confuse the suggestions of the evil spirit with the invitations of the Holy Spirit. Thus enters sin which interrupts the ascent toward God and excludes the creature from the city of God. There is no fault of man which is limited to a pure act of the will detached from all else. One or another creature, through sin, is turned from its end: by the inclination of the feelings, the body, exterior riches, other men. Sin profanes man and, with him, a portion of the world.

So Christ has put at the disposition of His Church another sacrament which arouses in man this new beginning which is penance. He is reestablished in the friendship of God and directed toward his end. At the same time, he takes up the creature which was the occasion and instrument for his sin to lead it again toward God, but with a note of sorrow conferred by the reparation or satisfaction inherent in penitence. We must speak of these things later (cf. chapter nine).

The life of the Christian here below develops not according to a regular line of ascent, but with certain ups and downs. His intelligence and his will, though enlightened by faith and vivified by charity, are incapable of embracing in a single act all the creatures associated with him to place them in the divine city. These powers act sporadically. They must recover many times. He finds within himself also, in the course of spiritual growth, weak points where temptation may easily creep in. He can fall into the rupture of mortal sin, but more frequently into the retardations of venial sin. In both cases, an influx of grace permits a new start. The sacrament of Penance is the instrument ordained to confer it. We shall see later that the Church offers many other means of atoning for venial sin.

By this fact, Christian life tends to take on a rhythmic structure. But this rhythmic structure is more natural to man than the possibility of sin. It is in man's very being that he develop on the natural plane in a patterned period of activity and rest. And this same human nature serves to support the divine life; even more, it is permeated by it. So the accomplishment of the human vocation, the progressive consecration of the world to God, also takes place according to the rhythm of human duration. Christ gave us a sacrament closely related to this rhythm. It is the Eucharist. Like all the sacraments, it has two aspects: it is an instrument of worship rendered to God in, through, and with Christ; it is also an instrument of sanctification for men and of reparation for sin. This latter aspect makes men worthy of being introduced into the sacrifice of Christ and thus consecrated to God, and finally of entering into the mystery of the Holy Trinity. We shall not return to the first of these aspects, but we must stress the second here. The Eucharist is food which repairs our powers and makes us grow; it is also a remedy that cures. It is given by the Church in the name of Christ to be completely centered in human life. It is at the summit of that elementary structure of life, the week. All terrestrial activity begins and ends on Sunday. On this day, the first in dignity, man enjoys what he has gained and makes it his own in the peace and quiet of contemplation. At the same time, he concentrates his forces to gain new energy and run another lap. The eucharistic banquet elevates the natural meaning of all this and so should become for the Christian, in view of accomplishing his divine mission, as necessary and unforgettable as nourishment for the body. The Church does even more. She inserts the Eucharist in the elementary rhythm of life marked out by the alternation of days and nights. The Mass is the culminating point of the day toward which all Christian activity aims and from which all flows.

Thus the Christian, each Sunday or even each day, receives this divine nourishment and from it a new abundance of charity. Thanks to this he can lead each creature he contacts in the course of his daily labors into unity with Christ. The world, however, is hard to penetrate. God is no longer clearly visible in it; it absorbs human forces; one easily falls back on too natural a plane. A spiritual hunger disturbs the soul faithful to the Lord, it needs recourse to Christ in order to find in Him the source of all perfect action in the world. In Communion, Christ configures the one who receives Him. In the course of time an interaction between Christ and the world takes place through the experience of the Christian. The Christian goes into the world carrying the message of Christ. He tries to instill this message; but at the same time he has to live like his neighbors. This profane life engulfs him and if he would not soon be submerged in it, he must hasten back to Christ, but with new human experience. He then comes to compare his experiences with the perfect model of all human existence, to purify it by his contact with Christ. Then he returns to his milieu of life, but better equipped to enter and sanctify it. Thus the Christian leaven continually influences the world and introduces into it little by little the kingdom of heaven. Every human role in the world is vivified thanks to the sacraments of Penance and the Eucharist.

But more serious situations require a special influx of grace. Such is the menace of the danger of death. This is not the danger of violent death which the Christian has to meet with the graces of Confirmation, but the mortal danger of a sickness. At the end of life, the soul finds itself burdened by the weight of past sins; they have been forgiven, but the soul no longer has its sights fixed clearly on the goods of eternity; perhaps the spirit does not have a pure enough faith because the passing life still attracts it. The less eternal life is manifest in any sensible way, the more death appears as an annihilation of this earthly life. Moreover, the body is weakened by illness, its energies are spent. Then it is that the sufferer must assume a new role; he finds himself at the very threshold of the passage from death to life. He must receive a final configuration to Christ, such as He expressed on the Cross in the Psalm: "My God, My God, why have You forsaken Me?" [8] The tragic issue of this contrast: all created supports fall away as the soul seeks in vain for something to lay hold of; but all is accomplished in a total submission to the Father: this is the consummation of the consecration of the world to God. The sufferer threatened by death experiences the stages marked by the four last words of Christ from the Cross: the abandonment of all human aid: "My God, My God . . ."; the exhaustion of physical forces: "I thirst"; the fulfillment of offering the world to God: "It is consummated"; and: "Father, into Thy hands I commend My spirit." [9]

Note that the sacrament of the anointing of the sick is closely related to the situation of the patient. Indeed, the final efficacy of the sacrament is purification from all trace of sin, as we shall explain. However, the prayers which precede and follow the anointings speak only of strengthening and of curing the illness. It seems to us that the liturgical meaning is a request for the return of health, the situation of the patient before death being such a grave peril that one can only pray that the danger be taken away. Implicitly there is also a request for the graces necessary to meet whatever situation results.

Two other sacraments are related to the beginning of life. One is concerned with supplying the very source of the divine life in the world. This is the sacrament of Orders. The other is concerned with terrestrial life, the sacrament of Matrimony. He who receives the sacrament of Orders assumes a position of capital importance in the Church. He is conformed to Christ in a special way; he becomes a participant in His priesthood; in him is imprinted a character which enables him to make present in the world the sacrifice of Christ with all the grace it contains. Here we find ourselves in the heart of man's mission to consecrate the world to God. It is a role so lofty that it requires a special influx of grace, a special motion of the Holy Spirit to make the subject capable of being Christ's instrument and of assuming the responsibility for the Christian people, the body of Christ. This grace and the sacerdotal character confer on the man who receives them a new consecration which places him henceforth apart from the laity. But this is not the object of our study. If we have, however, mentioned the sacrament of Orders, it is to show its relation to the other sacraments; it is also because the layman ought also to see its place and value in relation to his own proper role in the Church.

There is another fundamental role in the Mystical Body. It is that created by marriage. It has to do with the life of the primary call of society, not just on the natural plane, but in the Church. The spouses, through the sacrament, become instruments of grace for one another and their union finds fulfillment in their children. This union also affects all civil society and the ecclesial community through the bonds which naturally link it to its milieu.

We must speak of the new grace attached to marriage. The spouses are changed by the Holy Spirit, not just as individuals who have to assure their personal salvation—with, it is true, the entire relationship this salvation has to the others in their milieu—but as members of a stable community. Every grace received, and thus every action of charity, is social by nature, meaning *it is for* the person responsive to the other, both striving toward a superior end which will increase them. First in order of their love is their child, then their neighbor. This sacrament, unlike Orders, does not confer a character, for the grace of marriage does not look to divine worship; and, besides, it is attached to the terrestrial community which the spouses form and which in eternity will be reabsorbed into the community of Christ's body. Its stability is relative to life here below. However, it is necessary to insist on the permanence of the right to this grace. Throughout their lives, the spouses must draw on it, one for the other; but this grace is given in accord with the person's free acceptance.

For laymen living in the world, the family is the hearth to which all human activities naturally converge. Here they are taken up both individually and in common with the other members, and here they receive that primary sanctification which renders them capable of entry into the kingdom in and by the sacrifice of Christ.

First there are the personal activities of the two spouses, all that contributes to the development of one or the other on the physical, intellectual, and moral planes. They reflect one to the other their thoughts, sentiments, tendencies, mutually enlightening each other and helping each other to grow humanly and divinely. Together they advance toward the eternal kingdom. There is also the task of educating the children; here again, different points of view as well as diverse functions permit, in loving exchange, as balanced as possible a development of each of the children. Then there are the outside activities on the professional and social levels, in the civic and political milieus. Finally, there is the commitment, both individual and together, in the ecclesial community. On all these levels, the joint action in the home renders even more fruitful this sanctifying action which runs through all human life.

We said: *normally*. All we can do here is outline an ideal. But we have to take note of the wounds of sin. The union of the spouses tends constantly to its perfection but it can arrive only at a proximate perfection. The adaptation of one to the other, the mutual opening up takes place sometimes only slowly, and it is necessary to be aware of all the personal and social factors: temperaments and characters do not harmonize at the first instant. One can have social commitments in the world or in the Church which the other does not understand very well; sometimes these matters must be put off until later or the spouse must accept them without clear understanding. Even more, harmony sometimes has to remain enveloped in a mystery never to be clarified here below, such as when the relationship with another requires a professional secrecy to guarantee respect for the other person.

We must note certain trials also: illness or moral weaknesses. In spite of all, the home will remain fruitful through faithfulness in the sacrifice and suffering of reparation. This is not the place to consider this aspect implied in all Christian life and inherent in the consecration of the world. We shall return to it in a later chapter.

Here is the last reservation. This role of the married layman is normal for the majority, yet it is necessary to envisage vocations to celibacy in the world. Here too we see the life of ordinary members of the Mystical Body, drawn to a special degree of perfection, but without the need for intervention of a special sacrament. We shall discuss the means at their disposal later on.

Yet, the sacramental efficacy of the Church is not limited to the seven sacraments. The entire Church is herself a vast sensible sign of grace, she is herself a sacrament. The Church is the kingdom of God establishing itself visibly on earth. Therefore, she offers to men who adhere to Christ by faith and who will to become a part of that kingdom an activity that prefigures eternal life.

This is only a prefiguring. This fact must be underscored. The Church is not the city of God already completed, which is to be juxtaposed to the city of earth—two cities given to unrelenting battle until one is destroyed and the other has completely supplanted it. Rather, it is necessary to represent the heavenly Jerusalem as descending from heaven [10] to be "the dwelling of God with men" [11] and to "make all things new" [12] by penetrating the terrestrial realities. This renewal is a progressive thing. Thus the Church here below is not totally visible. However, she has a human-divine visible structure established principally by the sacraments linked to the center of the Church, the sacrifice of Christ. Everywhere in the living body of the earthly Church, the divine life flows invisibly. Christians, living members of this body, form a network in which charity circulates. In certain instances, this life comes forth in visible signs: in the sacraments. But everywhere else, it also tends to manifest itself sensibly by penetrating earthly realities and making them pass from the profane domain into the divine by bringing about their consecration to God. For this, the Church proposes to her children certain attitudes or certain ways of utilizing these earthly objects in a divine manner; she presents them with examples, models which will dispose them to receive grace through their human activities.

Among these types, some are very near to the kingdom, to such a degree that they are already part of it. We can place in this first category all the rites and liturgical actions that surround the Mass and the essentials of the sacraments. These are prayers, actions, benedictions, exorcisms. At the same time, the Church prescribes the use of diverse objects to support the ardor of the soul. Because these rites prepare for, underline, or develop the effect of the sacraments, they were long designated by the same word. Then, for the sake of precision, from the twelfth century on, they were distinguished with the name *sacramentals*. Canon law defines them: "things or actions which the Church regularly uses, by way of a sort of imitation of the Sacraments, to obtain by her prayers effects especially of a spiritual nature." [13]

During liturgical celebrations, the Christian people truly live in a spiritual milieu of the Church, all are carried toward the Lord by the motion of the entire Church; they experience partially for some moments a human life fully consecrated to God. Are not such the reflections one gathers from the lips of the faithful after the particularly fervent celebration of a Paschal Vigil, following an adult Baptism in which the exorcisms and other rites were religiously carried out and a few words of explanation were given, or simply after the celebration of Mass in a community where all were of one heart and one soul?

There are also the "advance guards" of the Church in the midst of the profane world. These are consecrated persons or blessed objects. The Church, by this consecration, confers on them an orientation toward the last end, which is God, so that the persons themselves thus consecrated, or those with whom they are associated, or those who use these objects, are aided in turning creatures to God. Such is the consecration of a virgin, or a chalice, or an altar. Such is the blessing of candles on Candlemas or the blessing of palms. These too are sacramentals, but in an isolated state instead of being part of a liturgical whole.

We must add here the prayers which the Church proposes for all sorts of needs: litanies for harvests, prayers to express varied requests. The piety of our contemporaries is not inclined toward this type of devotion. But the laity thus deprive themselves of a precious help for the accomplishment of their tasks. This general disaffection results especially from the fact that the meaning of religious gestures and attitudes has been lost. In fact, as soon as their role and signification are put in their true light, the ancient use of them returns. Such has been the case with the use of holy water since the restoration of the paschal liturgy in which its relationship with Baptism is clearly seen.

It is also important to understand how they achieve their purpose. The definition from canon law cited above is sufficiently explicit. The sacramentals and all the practices approved by the Church which are related to them do not produce grace. Such an instrumental efficaciousness is reserved to the sacraments. Here the effect is obtained by way of supplication. For all human situations or activities, the Church offers her aid. She takes up the human object and the action. By words and signs related to them, she puts on the lips of men a prayer of supplication that these creatures may indeed be directed toward the Lord, beyond the earthly end they envision. It follows that the blessing will attach to this creature a constant reminder of supplication which will incline God to give His grace and to stir in man an impulse toward the kingdom of heaven in the course of the activity thus accomplished. It should go without saying that this effectiveness does not exist unless the man who uses these blessings is in his soul disposed to the grace and is attentive, inasmuch as possible, to conform himself to the orientation the Church attaches to the creature. Thus putting one's hand into holy water does not have a magic efficacy. It is rather a prayer by action, extremely short, by which one asks God to prolong the purifying effect of Baptism in the action or creature which is now present. An airplane or any machine, once blessed, is not in itself an instrument of grace; but the blessing conferred on it is a supplication attached as it were to the object. Its purpose is that each time man makes use of it, he feels an attraction to use it for good. We can see that the Christian who lives by faith voluntarily has recourse to these means for aid in all the concrete circumstances of his life, and to better accomplish the consecration of the world to God.

Only those who are responsible for the direction of the Church have the power to propose to Christians sacramentals and associated practices. In effect, Christ gave them the power to act in His name. It is to Christ, the Head of the Church, that they go to find their inspiration. In Him is found the perfect example of all that the members of His body must accomplish in time and of the perfect prayer to address to God. It is not necessary to picture this example in a material way, as if Christ had performed the acts and pronounced the words which the Church institutes under the form of sacramentals. It is necessary to picture this source of all the life of the Church's body in Christ as the intuition of an artistic genius which is afterwards expressed in the varied forms of art. At various times in history, the Church, inspired by the Spirit, has presented her children with certain rites to use in order to approach favorably profane creatures.

In these historic junctures, there is a completely human element which marks the attitude of the Church. Thus we have here but *prefigurations* of the kingdom of God. And here we use this word in a second sense. They are not just fragmentary helps, but they are also enticements to make the kingdom of God penetrate progressively into the world. So we should not be surprised if the ways of acting proposed by the Church are not the best suited to all times; they are in some way dependent on circumstances. We see, for example, in a given age, that the Church was very favorable to eucharistic devotion under the form of exposition and benediction of the Blessed Sacrament, while in our days these practices are limited so as to favor rather the liturgical celebration of the Mass. But in one case as in the other, the Church is concerned with giving all possible help to the laymen in the world.

Finally, it is necessary to speak of portions of the world acquired for the kingdom and already organized in some way. We wish thus to designate the structures of every nature proposed or accepted by the Church which more or less completely embrace human activities and integrate them in different degrees into the kingdom. Among exterior structures, it is necessary to enumerate the different associations of Catholic Action grouped about the parish or organized in more extensive movements; then, penetrating more into the spiritual, the different types of pious unions among which one might, for example, name the Legion of Mary; then the confraternities; finally the societies and orders which are properly religious. Here also the Church proposes ways for action which aid in the consecration of the creature to God. But this is a point which would require special development. Here we only mention it.

FOOTNOTES:

1 Eph. 2, 19.

2 Rom. 8, 17.

3 Rom. 8, 16.

4 I Cor. 15, 22.

5 I Cor. 2, 6.

6 I Cor. 2, 15.

7 Cf. also I Cor. 3, 1–3, and Heb. 5, 12–14.

8 Ps. 21, 2.

9 Mt. 27, 46; Jn. 19, 28–30; Lk. 23, 46.

10 Ap. 21, 2.10.

11 Ap. 21, 3.

12 Ap. 21, 5.

13 *"Sacramentalia sunt res aut actiones, quibus Ecclesia, in aliquam sacramentorum imitationem, uti solet ad obtinendos, ex sua impetratione, effectus praesertim spirituales"* (Can. 1144). Cf. St. Thomas, *S. Th.,* I–II, q. 108, a. 2, ad 2; II–II, q. 99, a. 1; III, q. 65, a. 1, ad 3, 6, 8; III, q. 71, a. 3 especially ad 2.

6

Receiving the Word of God

By participating in the sacrifice of Christ and by using the sacraments, the Christian works to transform the world and to consecrate it to the Lord. He does this on his own free initiative, for the marvelous instruments of redemption and of grace have no magic or blind efficacy. Man deals with them in the light, an indispensable condition for free conduct. God Himself has furnished this light. He has spoken to make known His plan of salvation. The reception of this word is, then, indispensable for participation in the realization of this plan. It is necessary, on the one hand, to listen attentively to this word in order to enter into the plan. It is also necessary to assimilate it in order to be able to then communicate it to the world.

The layman who has taken cognizance of his vocation as a Christian in the world meets here a double necessity. First, empowered by his baptismal character to enter into the redemptive mystery of the Mass in order to bring to it, along with himself, the offerings of creatures, he is called to know Him who is both the priest and victim of this unique sacrifice. For this mystery into which he is introduced is a mystery of love, and there is no love without knowledge of the person loved. Thus it is indispensable for the Christian, even for the least of the faithful who has no charge in the direction of the Church, to discover who Christ is and what the divine mysteries are. The essentials of this knowledge are given to the faithful in the form of current religious instruction: catechism, lessons in religion, doctrinal sermons or conferences.

Nevertheless, this primary need is more extensive than that. It is necessary to enter into personal contact with the Lord in the course of the sacrifice of the Mass. Theoretical notions about religion like those of the Greeks or the Romans are useless. One must drink from the very source of God's message consigned to Holy Scripture and given in a living way by the Church. This reception of the message takes place in living faith through charity. But this is possible only in a religious context which implies respectful attention, adoration, and prayer, the very manner in which the Church listens to Jesus her Spouse. Each Christian, being a member of the Mystical Body, should participate in this attitude of receiving the word of God.

Within the body, it is necessary to discern divers functions. According to the greater or lesser degree in which the members participate in the hierarchical duties, the need of hearing the Word is greater or less. Certainly the heads of the Church, the successors of the apostles, have the greatest responsibility. They have the mission to "guard the good trust through the Holy Spirit, who dwells in us." [1] This task is closely bound up with that of making present the redemptive mystery in all times and places.

Laymen have their own responsibility. Since they have to participate actively in the sacrifice of the Mass offered for them, they must also receive the Word personally. Passivity is no longer admissible in either case. The word of God is proclaimed. That it be really received, a completely interior activity must intervene made up of reflections, petitions for light, requests for application of the Word in one's life. These acts need not, however, be made explicit. A very simple interior attitude can contain them all; this attitude can be well enough summarized as an *opening up of the soul* to the Lord.

Here we touch on that aspect of *growth* proper to the Christian life. It is not sufficient to know approximately who Jesus is and what the Christian mysteries are. This is a contact of love, and love cannot remain at rest. It does not cease to strive for a more perfect knowledge of the beloved. This knowledge of Christ and the mysteries is contained in the very message of God. Thus ceaseless searching is needed, continual delving into Scripture.

The spirituality of the layman is then a far cry from what many Christians think, Christians who are content with elementary instruction received from the catechism and who use the pretext of many occupations to excuse themselves from deepening their knowledge. On the other hand, it is necessary to guard against a certain intellectualism which is satisfied by a curious study of religious problems outside of any religious context.

The Church, however, in the liturgy, assures her faithful of all that is necessary on this subject. This is the place to recall that the word of God should be received from the Church herself who gives it in a living way, that is, in relation to both the mystery celebrated and the circumstances of human life. Reading the Scriptures for oneself and hearing them proclaimed by the Church in the first part of the Mass are two very different things. In this last case, they are grouped, related with other passages, whence comes a new light to clarify the mystery about to be celebrated. Also, they are surrounded by prayer: the orations; we add here also the meditations designated by the names Responsory, Gradual, Tract: these are the Scripture texts themselves which are taken, repeated, and become food for the soul. A certain dialogue with the faithful is expressed by the invitation: "The Lord be with you," which reminds the layman that he cannot remain passive.

It goes without saying that the proclamation of the word in the liturgy is not final. The Christian is not asked to be content with hearing the texts used in the liturgical celebration. On the contrary, there is an appeal to go to the context, to read and meditate on the Biblical books themselves from which these excerpts have been taken. But this personal meditation is to be illumined by the same light of faith stirred up by the Church; it should be surrounded, as in the course of the liturgy, with this same atmosphere of prayer. God Himself is speaking, and we listen as servants called to live with Him as friends.

Group research of a religious character can be most helpful in this. The Biblical study groups which are springing up everywhere in the Christian world are a powerful help and are usually endowed with this indispensable double character of attentive study and religious respect. The contemporary Biblical and liturgical renewals too have been an important element in the spirituality of laymen. They favor this personal awareness of the treasures of revelation which are confided to each member of the Mystical Body and closely linked to spiritual maturity.

This double renewal also facilitates the response to the second need of the lay vocation in the world. If the layman can participate in the sacrifice of Christ with his whole being and with all the creatures he deals with, it is supposed that he has already worked for the transformation of these creatures and of the powers of his own being, that whole complex which makes up the world, thus to make an offering worthy of the Lord. We have already mentioned how the sacraments and their extensions, the sacramentals, are the channels which carry grace into the world and make possible the consecration of the world to God. Even in this, this divine work can take place only if preceded by light.

We also said that the sacraments are appropriate to new situations which modify the course of human life; they are instruments of divine intervention to assimilate these situations. Yet it is necessary to see these situations in a true light, which can be none other than that of faith. But it is the word of God that furnishes this light, and here also the liturgical use of texts is significant. The Church has chosen them under the influence of the Holy Spirit in relation to the mystery being enacted. Those who are invested with the ministerial priesthood, in accomplishing these rites, relate this word and explain it. Those who use the sacraments receive this same word and seek to bring it into the situation in which grace is to work for the transformation of this portion of the world. Lively faith gives the sacrament its power of penetration by receiving the word. Faith, aided by the word, brings to light the true aspect of this human situation, which is to be sanctified.

Take Baptism, for example, in its original context in the paschal liturgy. The mystery in which the catechumen is to take part is underlined by the fundamental text of Saint Paul: "For we were buried with Him by means of Baptism into death, in order that, just as Christ has arisen from the dead through the glory of the Father, so we also may walk in newness of life. For if we have been united with Him in the likeness of His death, we shall be so in the likeness of His resurrection also. For we know that our old self has been crucified with Him, in order that the body of sin may be destroyed, that we may no longer be slaves to sin. Thus do you consider yourselves also as dead to sin, but alive to God in Christ Jesus." [2]

The rite will make this mystery present. The interpenetration of human and divine life, obtained by Christ's incarnation and redemption, will be realized for this man. The divine life reestablishes the life of man in a new situation by means of this rite of being plunged into the water, and this rite is rendered significant and efficacious by the almighty word of Christ. The baptized is helped to receive this word with faith by the entire meaningful context which enlightens it, the Scripture text, and the liturgical development found in the admirable preface for the consecration of baptismal water.

Under this aspect of the light of faith, we can find like considerations in the case of the other sacraments. For a final example, take marriage. The union of man and woman and the role of their life together which will follow are elevated to a new state by a participation in the mystery of the union between Christ and the Church. Here the text of the Epistle to the Ephesians gives the light: "Let wives be subject to their husbands as to the Lord; because a husband is head of the wife, just as Christ is head of the Church, being Himself Savior of the body. . . . Husbands, love your wives, just as Christ also loved the Church, and delivered Himself up for her. . . . This is a great mystery—I mean in reference to Christ and to the Church." [3] Thus the intelligence is enlightened by the light of faith and the will is attracted by charity, so that, little by little, in this human situation of marriage, a more and more perfect identification with the mystery of the union between Christ and the Church is realized. Here we look upon the living efficacy of the sacrament enlightened by the word in view of the consecration of the world to God.

As in the course of the Mass, the word of God proclaimed by the Church in the liturgy of the sacraments is an invitation to an incessant striving after light. It concerns the descent of the mystery of God into the world, a mystery which the faithful must receive. Each of the sacraments reveals an aspect of this mystery in relation to a given situation. But these aspects ought to come closer and closer together or at least to tend toward the establishment of the unique city of God. This does not come about without a deepening of the word of God with the aid of all the forms of instruction in the Church.

The sanctification of the world is progressive. We shall envision this in more detail in the following chapter when treating the stabilization of this consecration by means of the virtues, but here we must emphasize the efficacious role of the word of God in realizing this enduring transformation. It is not a question of establishing a balanced human world or a sort of golden age such as pagan legends imagine. For that, it would suffice to organize a society in which all human moral virtues would rule harmoniously. But here, the world must reflect Christ. The layman involved in the world must, then, enter more and more into his divine model to reproduce Him in his personal earthly experience. This does not mean a servile imitation of the attitudes, actions, and words of Christ. The situations are not the same as those which Jesus lived historically. They are analogous. Thus a transposition is necessary.

For example, the beauty of poverty and Christ's invitation to renounce the goods of the earth should be understood in relation to the concrete situation of each individual. This understanding belongs to the layman in the world. To him is given the grace to know and plumb the nature of his human situation. But this human situation must be purified, sanctified in order to be transformed finally in the consecration to the Lord. So the layman will make an appeal to the word of God which the Church gives him in a living way.

Let us insist on this last point for it is of extreme importance. The word of God, source of the light of faith, will not be just one or another text from Scripture which the layman himself will seek out to enlighten his conduct. Periodically we meet, in the course of Church history, reformers who pretended to return to pure faith. But they took the words of Scripture as human words, separating them from the mystery of the Church and from the divine mystery in which they are rooted. Thus Tertullian and the Montanists went astray in the first centuries, or the Albigensians and the Cathari in the Middle Ages; and so it is with many members of contemporary sects.

The word of light will not even be the interpretation of certain clerics or even theologians giving their own personal opinions. It has happened that experimental exegesis has returned to the sources, and sought the meaning of Scripture texts with the aid, indeed, of all the lights of science, but disregarding all the reflection Christians have applied to them through the centuries. This is to transpose to the religious plane the spirit recently prevalent in manuals of history and philosophy: to believe them, philosophical thought, born among the Greeks, disappeared during the night of the Middle Ages to be reborn among the moderns with Descartes.

The unique word of God which we can hear is that pronounced by the Church. For the Church is the total body of Christ including, first of all, the Head Himself, Christ. This body has lived throughout the centuries since the coming of Jesus. To perceive the light contained in this life of the Church, much attention and a profound humility are necessary. Growth projects the truths of the Gospel into human reality; a sort of maturation sets free all the dimensions of the truth enclosed at first in the seed. The magisterium of the Church has intervened to explain and make precise certain aspects of these truths, but others remain as yet unformulated. We need not hurry, outside the magisterium, to set off the truth in these concise formulas. That would run the risk of abridging them. Thus the layman will make his appeal to the teaching of the Church in its totality.

But he must, for his part, strengthened by this light, confront the present world. Nobody can understand the problems of present-day humanity as the layman can. These problems are of every kind, and each person must pay special attention to those which pertain to his professional specialty. But at the same time, he must not be too exclusive, for an analytic study is without value if it is not surrounded by a comprehensive view of things.

It is as a Christian that the layman meets the world. All his human abilities are put in play, but according to a certain spirit. It is impossible to consider an object by making a picture of it omitting certain details and leaving out a primary theory or hypothesis concerning it. In addition to the word of God, Christian wisdom, formed from all the reflection of past ages, should aid the layman to purify his spirit so that he may preserve only those preconceptions suited to a better understanding of the real and disarm himself of those prejudices which deform him and render him incapable of finding solutions to improve the world and transform it according to the plan of God. Unconsciously, man's thoughts are easily left open to the philosophical prejudices permeating the mentality of the age. In our age, for example, there is the danger of being contaminated by the views of historical determinism emanating from Marxism. This is what recently compromised the "Jeunesse de l'Eglise" (Young People of the Church) movement.

So it is necessary to accept a certain spiritual analysis. This is possible only by constant recourse to the light of the Church. On the other hand, the layman is not to despise his own abilities. He must gradually make his contributions at the necessary points. He does this only through continual exchange between the experience of the world and the light of the Church. He hesitates, he tries, he sometimes fails, but he must be dominated by a real humility which keeps him aware of his weakness and of the possibility of error, and by an exact docility to both human facts and to the light received from the Church. It seems to us that this latter is a trait characteristic of the spirituality of the Christian layman. He must never abandon one or the other of these two points of support.

We shall now treat especially the role of the layman in society, a role thanks to which the Mystical Body of Christ develops in the world and gradually transforms moral life on the various personal, family, economic, social, professional, civic, and international levels. It must be said that this concerns a primary and most basic degree of sanctification.

The layman, though involved principally in the world, is not without responsibilities in the properly religious life of the Church. One of these resides in the reception of the divine light which stirs the progress of this religious life. Revelation ceased with the death of the last apostle, but the treasure of truths confided to the care of the leaders of the Church is continually enhanced. New aspects of it are manifested under the influence of the Holy Spirit. A sort of maturation brings this about in the entire body of the Church. We mentioned this maturation earlier in this chapter. The Holy Spirit does not work in the Pope and the bishops alone, but in those as well who are simply laymen. Without a doubt, strong personalities often have roles as initiators. The development of dogma is often accomplished under the impulse of those who are called "Fathers of the Church" or of certain theologians who are famous for their learning and holiness. Nevertheless, these initiatives develop in the midst of the entire people of the Church to the measure in which the faithful have shown themselves docile to the interior impulse of the Holy Spirit.

Thus it is that more and more popular devotional practices have been able to call the attention of the hierarchy to some truth up to now somewhat obscure. The dogma of the Immaculate Conception or the Assumption could be defined only after having been lived more or less obscurely by the entire body of the Church. This vitality diffused in the members of the body has been the primary condition for the awareness that these truths are part of the revealed deposit of truth.

This role of the body does not, however, replace the decision of the hierarchy. It is up to them to discern the true aspiration of the Spirit. It can happen that pious movements arise in the lone imagination of some devout person. It belongs solely to the leaders of the Church to judge the authenticity of the doctrine.

In addition, the Church's magisterium has a positive role. It is not content with confirming certain thoughts issuing from the spirit of some Christians. It is really the magisterium which affirms by a new judgment that such and such a truth is part of revelation. And this judgment is guided by the Holy Spirit.

Here again, the layman—whatever initiatives he was able to take previously—will now show his Christian spirit by a complete docility. If he is accustomed to search interiorly the word of God, as we have explained, then the light of faith will enlighten him, join the ardor of his charity, and dispose his spirit and his will to recognize in the plan of the Church the same divine inspiration which he follows within himself.

FOOTNOTES:

[1] 2 Tm. 1, 14.
[2] Rom. 6, 4-12.
[3] Eph. 5, 22-23.25.32.

7

Stabilization of Consecration
Through Virtues

To consecrate a creature to God means to transfer it from the profane world into the kingdom of God, that is, from an alienation from God to a divine belonging. Only grace can bring about this transformation, and Christ, the Head of the Mystical Body offered in sacrifice, is the source of that grace. The sacraments bring it into the fundamental situations of human existence, the sacramentals extend it into all human life.

Clearly grace, producing these effects, is not just exterior to the creature; it penetrates it profoundly. In particular, it stirs man to free acts, or rather to continued activity conformed to the "divine modes" mentioned in a preceding chapter. Thus these interior dynamisms, which we call virtues, develop. Through them, the consecration of the world receives a certain stability and the creature acquires a primary degree of sanctity.

The Christian cannot neglect the virtues, even the most humble moral virtues. The consecration of the world cannot be limited to a simple offering of the creature without changing this creature. The end of this consecration is God Himself, entry into the mystery of God. But this requires a configuration to God, which is the work of grace. It is also necessary for the creature to accept this action, but such acceptance takes place slowly, in proportion to the development of these virtues. A sort of mutual reaction takes place between the action of grace and the dynamism of the virtues. An influx of grace received with docility stirs virtue, and virtue (at the same time always accompanied and permeated by grace) disposes the subject for a new influx of grace, and so on.

By acquiring virtues, the Christian begins to transform the world. These dynamisms of which we speak do not leave the world unchanged. As soon as man begins to act, he adopts an approach toward the surrounding milieu; this establishes a certain type of relationship with reality. The very face of the world, because of this relationship, thus takes on determined characteristics. The objects man uses are not just extensions of his members, allowing him a greater range of action and greater efficiency. Rather man assigns to these objects a purpose, and often he orders them to his own satisfaction, his own pleasure, in a word, to himself. As these actions are repeated, this way of looking at and using the world becomes habitual. Thus he will regard the various dishes of his meal only as palatal pleasures, and this will be like an automatic perspective bound to a pleasure-seeking attitude. In his sight, others become his servants, instruments of his pleasure, agents for his profit, means to his personal ends. He centers the world more and more around himself, and his whole life becomes a series of ordered reactions, ready to make contact with objects.

But such an attitude toward the world, united with a collection of habitual ways of behaving in the world, has meaning not for the individual alone. My way of meeting the world influences that of my neighbor and of all others with whom I come into contact. In this way family or regional customs, even those of an entire generation, are created. We are expected to live in such and such a manner, to behave in a given way. On the other hand, there are things we just do not do, boundaries almost physically impossible to cross.

In this way, medieval forms of fasting, or varied forms of austerity, have become impossible in our day. This does not follow from a strictly intellectual rationalization. Its explanation is a social complex, solidly established, an almost insurmountable obstacle for those who would go against it, even if their own physical constitution would permit them to repeat the exploits of the ancient ascetics.[1]

Such attitudes and dynamisms with regard to the exterior world and the milieu of life modify reality. Because of these, we do not meet the world indifferently, rather we see it, perceive it, are prepared to act on it, in keeping with these primary dispositions.

Something similar happens when the layman, aided by grace, strives to consecrate the world to God. By acquiring virtues himself, he obtains for himself, and consequently for the social milieu he influences, dynamisms related to a particular view of things. He will, therefore, be inclined to use creatures in a manner that will bring them, along with himself, into the kingdom of God. For the virtues produce a configuration of the world to good, thus making things God-like by favoring a God-like manner of acting. Let us not forget that "as the substance of God is His action, the highest configuration of man to God is bound up with a certain operation." [2]

Human action in the world should begin by being good on the simple moral level. The Christian, for example, will strive to use the radio or the television moderately, in a way that will help him cultivate his tastes and relax. Physical exercise and sobriety will have their place in his life so that his spirit can sustain its efforts and free him from sensual attractions. This is the action of stable habits, vivified by grace. If this Christian be the head of a family and if all the family's members have like views, a family spirit is created, permeated with the virtue of temperance. And this same spirit, lived by a certain number of Christian families, spreads through society creating an attitude about eating habits, influencing the quality of radio and television programs, and bringing, finally, the sensible world to light, inclining men to approach it with moderation and austerity.

To look at the other side, we must develop similar considerations regarding the active virtues. The world is not made up solely of goods to be assimilated, but also of difficulties, of dangers which are sometimes deadly. Corrections and detours are necessary to attain, finally, the reign of harmony. Man cannot attain this end unless he is ready to hold firm in the midst of difficulties, to be patient in order to triumph over them, as well as to react strongly to overcome the obstacles. Virtues of this order create a climate of calm courage in the world, climate of firmness and self-possession which are elementary factors, but of fundamental importance for harmony and balance.

The Christian living in the world should not see these virtues of temperance and fortitude as did the ancient moralists, but in relation to the consecration of the world. The fundamental conditions for the possibility of this consecration are involved here. This consecration seeks the incorporation of the world, with man as its center, into the divine life. But this cannot take place without the giving of self in charity. It is by this that Christ brought us into the mystery of the Trinity. He delivered Himself for His own in order that they, in their turn, might accomplish the commandment He so uniquely exemplified. Here, in fact, is the entry into the life of the Trinity, which is the mutual giving of the Three Divine Persons.

But here on earth, the life of charity is carried on throughout all human activity, and these human activities utilize created realities. And so our way of viewing our approach to these realities must not be selfish. In other words, we must consider them with a spirit of detachment gained from good habits of temperance. Indeed, temperance will dispose us not to abuse material goods, but rather to live in poverty that these goods can become the material for the gift of charity. At the same time, the virtue of fortitude will guard against attachment to a personal complacency which makes us too ready to devote ourselves to the service of others, to the detriment of order in our personal, family, or social life.

But more important for the consecration of the world are the social virtues grouped around justice. Avoiding obstacles opposed to the communication of divine life is not their only purpose. These virtues are, in effect, preliminaries to the life of charity. It is not necessary to set up an artificial opposition between justice and charity. If, indeed, justice strives to render to each his due, then it disposes us to recognize the dignity of the other's person and to work for the establishment of a society in which each may find the free development of his personality.

Let us not forget that charity, which is essentially the love of friendship, is possible only among equals. To make men able to enter into His intimacy, God raised them to a divine life and made them sons in His unique Son. At the same time, this life of charity cannot spread through the world unless Christians recognize in each of their fellow human beings the same dignity as they find in themselves, regardless of the accidental differences of condition, class, or race. But this can be no mere theoretical recognition. It involves many concrete requirements. We must accord to others on the familial, professional, economic, political, and international levels the rights which flow from this dignity. Thus we can see how deep-rooted are these social duties of the layman in the world. His vision of society always centers on the perspective of the consecration of the world to God.

The attitudes suggested by the virtues related to justice, we must add, prepare for justice in the strict sense. Certain of these virtues color the duties rendered to others, inasmuch as they are rendered to relatives, to leaders of some dignity, or to benefactors. Others have the task of establishing harmony among the current relationships in society. First of all, loyalty is the basis of all relationships; there is also that friendly attitude which establishes a kind of elementary friendship and is called affability. Finally, there are those virtues which exclude all inhumane firmness and hardness in the applications of justice, e.g., liberality and equity.

Let us now imagine a society of men who are continually led by these stable good habits and permeated with charity in all their personal and social actions, in all their cultural, familial, professional, and civic activities. They act with the intuitive delicacy that suggests Christian prudence in every action. We would already have a mirror of the kingdom of heaven, this earthly city reflecting the city of God. One step more, offering this earthly city to the Triune God and His acceptance of it, would accomplish the final transformation of this temporal world into the world of eternal happiness.

But everything here below takes place slowly, step by step. We cannot hope that this perfect harmony will be realized before the termination of human history. For all that, however, we cannot think that the offering to God and the passage into the kingdom of God is to be put off until the time of this total achievement. This offering is continually renewed to maintain in all creatures a fundamental orientation toward God. And the virtue, which finally establishes the consecration of the world to God, is the virtue of religion.

This virtue commands the religious attitude of every man at

every instant. Let us not represent the virtues as acting one after the other in a sort of succession or juxtaposition. They are all related and their actions are unified. Religion, in particular, must be continually in action, for we must never lose sight of the fact that man is made for God and that he must go to Him with all creation. As a Christian, he knows that the God toward whom he strives wants to make him His beloved son. This conviction is translated into acts which are essentially interior. There is first the act called "devotion," not taken in its ordinary sense, but in its full theological meaning of renewed disposition toward God. The act we are talking about is not to be confused with exterior actions, which always imply a succession marked by interruptions, but it is something of a permanent disposition of the soul toward God; or, at least, such ought to be the final effect of the virtue of religion. Through the virtue of religion all exterior actions, those human actions we spoke of above, redirected by the moral virtues, become the material of a constant interior offering.

This prolonged act of disposition or of devotion is accompanied by prayer, which is a petition addressed to God to obtain all that is necessary for the final consecration of self and of creatures. The prayer of the layman will be characterized by a certain accent placed on the transformation of the world; it will also be marked by daily contact with the misery of men and will find its best expression in the second part of the *Our Father* with its confident prayer for deliverance from evil. To sustain perfectly the return to God, this prayer tends to become constant. Ejaculatory prayers, which frequently crop up in the most absorbing occupations and which mount toward God like blazing shafts, are a happy approach to this ideal.

But these interior acts are stimulated and sustained by special exterior acts. True, every human action can serve for this offering, but since man's complete attention is required for this offering and its perfection, particular acts are needed whose unique purpose is to express devotion and interior prayer. This is the purpose of sacrifices, acts of adoration, prayers of praise. Here we come back to the liturgy. It offers the individual the necessary framework for weaving his own intimate religious life into that of the Church.

We alluded to the slow and fragmentary character of the consecration of the world to God. These moral virtues are an ideal. They are realized, even among the best of us, only very imperfectly. Is the vocation of the layman then defeated? Not at all. We must never forget that the Christian is a member of the Church, and the Church is the living body of Christ, continually growing from the coming of Jesus on earth until the end of time. The layman is part of this development, and his action on the world has meaning only by reason of its insertion into the heart of Christian time. By faith he attaches himself to Christ, who is the Head and ideal example of His body; and hope leads him to that terminus where the body will find its perfection in Christ, who will come to take final possession of His kingdom. Thus he can present himself in the sacrifice of the Mass with imperfect human accomplishments, even though they are marked by all sorts of weaknesses of which he himself is unaware. He makes his offering, as we have said, in a religious spirit of total abandonment into the hands of the Lord. And Christ "informs" it with His own offering, with all the perfection which will be realized throughout Christian time included in it. The value of this offering comes from the divine charity on which it is based, and divine charity is pure grace conferred by the Spirit of love. All that is required of us is a simple attitude of acceptance.

Note well, we do not mean to devaluate the task which properly belongs to man. The layman in the world cannot be content with a disembodied intention. He must take part in

Christ's sacrifice by a personal and free act. But he is closely bound to earthly tasks, and he must accomplish his purpose through these.

In this light, virtue has a new dimension. It is the constantly renewed and improved image of the Church; and the Church is the faithful spouse whom Christ has reserved that she may be pure, without spot or wrinkle, prepared for perfect union with her Bridegroom.

FOOTNOTES:

[1] On the other hand, some young social sets cultivate the habit of substituting fruit juices for the alcoholic drinks recently so popular.

[2] *S. Th.,* I–II, q. 55, a. 2, ad 3.

8

Religious Structures, Prefigurations
of the Kingdom of God

Through the sacraments and the sacramentals, the grace of Christ's sacrifice motivates the Christian, and little by little the Christian transforms the world. The virtues stabilize this transformation. But this stabilization of the work of consecrating the world does not remain piecemeal. Organization begins to appear. The structures of the kingdom of God arise under the influence of the Holy Spirit and the Church, as the Church approves and incorporates them. Sometimes she creates them herself.

We have already mentioned these structures with regard to separation from the world. We were then treating their role as protections against the seductions of the world. But they are not just protections; they are formed of living elements interiorly unified and the organizations themselves have a life since they are permeated with grace. These are modes of social living regulated by a body of legal prescriptions and enlivened by a special spirit. This social framework more or less totally and strictly surrounds the life of the Christian. And so we have more or less advanced prefigurations of the city of God implanted in this world; the work of world-consecration to God begins to see partial fulfillment. We meet these in all the religious or spiritual organizations approved by the Church: in orders, congregations, institutes, and associations of every nature. Here we shall treat them only in reference to the help they can render the layman in his consecration of the world.

Why did they develop in the Church? If we examine their history, we can better understand the need they answered.

What did the disciples think of when Jesus mentioned the kingdom? This word stirred in them a nostalgia deep in the heart of every Jew for the restoration of the kingdom of Israel. But as Christ unfolded His teaching, the notion of this kingdom became more mysterious and the disciples began to sense its divine implications. When they later learned that Jesus had come to give them a share in the marvelous life of God, their search to establish a parallel life here on earth is quite understandable. They sought an earthly mode of life that would let them live this divine life constantly. This desire is already present at the moment of the transfiguration when Peter, cleansed by the joy of contemplation, exclaims: "Rabbi, it is good for us to be here. And let us set up three tents . . ." [1] This would be a return to that life which the ancients had lived with God in the desert, but in a very different intimacy. Philip's request betrays this same nostalgia for the heavenly life: "Lord, show us the Father and it is enough for us." [2]

After the Lord had ascended into heaven, this same deep desire continued to motivate the disciples. They anxiously awaited the return of the Lord, eager for the heavenly life; they were already living it in part here on earth. Saint Paul witnesses it: "We look not at the things that are seen, but at the things that are not seen. For the things that are seen are temporal, but the things that are not seen are eternal." [3] These realities from on high seem already planted here below, but a desire is unrealistic, for the transformation takes place slowly.

However, this is what the soul desires: "For we know that if the earthly house in which we dwell be destroyed, we have a building from God, a house not made by human hands, eternal in the heavens. And indeed, in this present state we groan, yearning to be clothed with that dwelling of ours from heaven." [4]

By the very reason of providential circumstances, a radical solution appeared: martyrdom. Nor is this an evasion of the world. Paradoxically, the Christian who accepts martyrdom, though it removes him completely from the world, acts on the world in the greatest possible way, for he lives the life of perfect charity. Thus the Church accomplishes her mission to transform the world. Saint Stephen's case is typical. Tradition has seen the conversion of Saul as the result of this martyrdom which he himself witnessed.[5]

Nevertheless, an extraordinary act was not sufficient to form the city of God. A living organism was needed. The first attempt at this was at Jerusalem. For the first time, the disciples tried to put the lessons of their Master into practice in a community organization. In two different passages, the Book of Acts draws a picture of this common life. It was based on two principles: first, a definite religious life in common: "And they continued steadfastly in the teaching of the apostles and in the communion of the breaking of the bread and in the prayers." [6] Second, a custom was started of giving their material wealth to the community: "And all who believed were together and held all things in common, and would sell their possessions and goods and would distribute them among all according as anyone had need." [7]

This was a prefiguration of the city of God. It generated a magnetic attraction. This community at Jerusalem was the living milieu for proclamation of the word of God. At the same time it exemplified the testimony of the disciples: "Now the multitude of the believers were of one heart and one soul, and not one of them said that anything he possessed was his own, but they had all things in common. And with great power the apostles gave testimony to the resurrection of Jesus Christ our Lord; and great grace was in them all." [8] And so the transformation of the world took place through contact with a community, and this community was established and made enduring by a complexus of social organization, all this completely within the life of the world.

Though it will always remain the prototype of life totally dedicated to God, and though the founders of religious orders have tried to imitate it, this first attempt ended in failure. The Christians in Jerusalem were soon in misery and Saint Paul was seeking aid for them from the other Churches. We should not be surprised to see the Church's strivings having more or less fortunate results. The action of the Holy Spirit does not stifle human initiative, nor does it do away with human weakness; it does not inspire actions of absolute perfection, but it does guard against false orientations. In this case, the general idea was good and reappears later in many religious institutions, but the scope of this first attempt was too vast, too premature.

After this attempt, more modest organizations of the kingdom were proposed. Throughout the entire history of the Church, we see two parallel movements that tend to merge. Both of these, each in its own way, offered the layman basic structures for apostolic activity, important aids in the consecration of the world. One of these was the communities set apart from the world. They offered him a scale model, but a complete one, of the city of God. There were men in the world, too, who began to lay out the rough outlines of this same city. Taking the materials of the world, they were building according to the model already set up apart from the world. But the solitary city, once solidly established, opened its gates; its inhabitants went out temporarily to take on some of the duties of the layman. They stimulated the Christians in the world to gradually transform it into the holy city. They came to teach the laws of this holy city.

Then, however, there was a rush to found veritable little Christian cities. This idea did not spring up immediately, for the plan was not at first clear in the Christian consciousness. The inspirations of the Holy Spirit follow the wanderings of human ways. So, until the Edict of Constantine, Christians formed communities relatively isolated from the world and its seductions so as to be as perfect an image of the kingdom of God as possible. The emperor's conversion occasioned an invasion of the profane world into the Church. The empire became nominally Christian, but, for all that, its social structures were not transformed. Paganism presented a danger of contamination for the city of God. So the city of God had again to be set up apart from the profane world.

At first, the attempts were sporadic. A number of ascetics sought an austere life far from the world in the Egyptian desert, but each was on his own. From their midst emerges the figure of Saint Anthony (+356). Note that at the beginning he did not completely abandon the common life of men. In a cabin near his village, he adopted the life of the poor, making his living through manual labor and inspiring this laborious life with continual prayer. He was living the life of a layman, just like any man in the world, but he sanctified it by austerity, simplicity, and abandonment of the superfluous and the useless. Prayer vested his life with divine splendor. From other ascetics he visited, Anthony learned a number of other practices to fortify this life: nocturnal vigils devoted to prayer and the meditative reading of Scripture, fasts and other ascetic exercises. Anthony pursued this mode of life in the desert. And so, even among these anchorites in the desert, structures of the monastic life were already forming as primary outlines of the kingdom of God. These ascetics communicated their experiences and so all, in much the same manner, realized a common ideal. Anthony, for his part, would consolidate this ideal during his twenty desert years of retreat and battle against the demons.

In the second phase of his life, he separated himself more completely from the common mode of human life, yet this did not impair the efficacy of his action on the consecration of the world. On the contrary, it became greater. He acted through the force of his example. At the end of these twenty years, he had acquired a new strength and a renown for sanctity which attracted men to him.

However, for the monastic life to have its greatest effect on the world, it had to undergo a new transformation. With Anthony and his followers, the structures of the city of God were only potential. Though the mode of life these anchorites lived exercised a powerful attraction, it could not be transposed into the world itself. Saint Pachomius instituted the monastic life, truly the image of the kingdom of God manifested in the desert. Pachomius began by gathering his disciples around him, giving them a rule, and establishing a vast organization. He grouped the monks in houses according to the trades they carried on for the good of the monastery: weavers, mat-makers, tailors, carpenters, bakers, cooks, gardeners, cowherds, infirmarians, etc. He built a city of poverty and charity whose every activity was sanctified by regular community prayers during the day and the night and consolidated by a promise of obedience to the head of the monastery.

Later founders of orders contributed to the perfecting of monasticism, but added nothing essential. Thus we see the city of God on earth anticipating the eschatological age. Saint Basil was the first to reinforce the communitarian character of this institution by stricter organization. He made the communities smaller to make the personal relationship between the superior and the monks effective, and to assure greater harmony in the community through strict obedience in realizing the common good.

This form of life continued to spread for centuries in the East: it remains even in our days the model of the religious life. From the end of the fourth century, it spread in the West too, principally because of Saint Cassian. After some time in the East learning about the life of the desert fathers, he became the great promoter of monastic life in the West.

We shall not treat here the form of religious life Saint Augustine instituted, for it offers spiritual structures to the cleric engaged in the Church's ministry, but not to the layman. It became the religious life of the canons and had a development parallel to that of the monastic religious life.[9]

Other spiritual masters made their contribution in the West. Noteworthy among these is Saint Caesarius of Arles. He inscribed a new and important element into the monastic tradition: that of stability. But it is really the rule of Saint Benedict that gave Western monks and the abbey their distinctive character. Its originality lies in the role it gives to the abbot. He governs the community with supreme authority, but, at the same time, he is the spiritual father. And so the interior formation the abbot gives the monks encourages free obedience. In his community, the abbot holds a position similar to that of the *paterfamilias* in the ancient Latin society or the lord in the small cities of the Middle Ages. Thus the abbey becomes an example of Christian relationships of dependence by making obedience interior. In place of a task fulfilled because of constraint, we find the spontaneous response to the appeal of the head who seeks the common good of the city. Through a sort of leaven aided by grace, the monasteries instilled in the social structures of medieval society the Christian concept of obedience.

Parallel to Benedictine spirituality, another current came from Ireland and permeated Christianity in the sixth century with the image of Saint Patrick and Saint Columban. A monasticism of a very severe character inspired the whole Irish population. This was the type of Christianity that converted them. It also brought about a development of penitential practices among these Christians, a practice soon to spread through medieval Christianity and play an important part in the sanctification of the world: frequent confession and the practice of reparatory penance. What had remained exceptional practices of hermits among the monks of the Orient passed into daily life as a means of sanctification and reparation. Penances were added to the devotional confessions. Then by a kind of logical growth, there was the development of indulgences. Thus a network of mutual charity wove itself through all of medieval humanity. We should not underestimate its importance.

All we have been considering has concerned the influence of strictly religious structures on the world of the laity. We must look at the other side too. Lay institutions and movements also served to sanctify the profane world, the habitual environment of men. After the establishment of the Christian empire, the emperor and all his local chiefs became aware that they too had a responsibility toward the eternal salvation of their subjects. And so political institutions served as instruments for the consecration of the world. This idea of the sacred function of political power lasted even after the Reformation with more or less fortunate results. Such as they were, we cannot deny that these institutions that formed the framework of medieval Christianity had a certain efficacy, especially when they were utilized by saintly princes like Louis IX of France.

There were other institutions closer to the people. First was the Order of Penitents. We can judge its place only if we see the value the Church put on it around the sixth century. It was made up of laymen who decided to do penance in the state of "conversion." Some lived in communities, some lived alone. They lived an austere life; their clothes were drab; they were assiduous in attending the divine office in the Church and in saying certain private prayers; they were committed to keep perfect chastity or, if married, continence. The third orders of the thirteenth century were derived from this order of penitents. Until that time, the penitents remained under the direction of the bishops. After that, there were two branches connected to the Franciscans and the Dominicans.

The guilds were much larger organizations. With these, we no longer have an institution which follows a monastic life in the world as we had in the previous case. The guilds sought to sanctify one of the layman's essential tasks, his profession. They differed according to the occupations and involved obligations suited to the consecration of this particular phase of profane life.

We still have to underline the Church's efforts in this age to Christianize an occupation which seemed most contrary to the prescriptions of the Gospel: military service. One attempt was the military orders made up of laymen. Some of these even admitted families, demanding only poverty.[10] Another attempt was chivalry. Its ideals sought to introduce peace into the violent world of the Middle Ages. They made use of feudal relations and developed a mystique of Christian loyalty along with a feeling of Christian solidarity.

Up to that time, life was carried on in a Christian atmosphere. The action of the Church permeated the entire social strata. But a new world was in the making and it was characterized by the progressive development of a lay spirit. Varied human activities escaped the Church's control and, one after another, gained their independence. Thereafter, a new manner of consecrating the world to God was needed. Up to now, the mode of consecration had been given from on high by the Church, but now it had to flow from the very milieu of lay life. In medieval Christianity, the structures for the stabilization of this consecration of created things formed outside the world in those models' of the heavenly city, the monasteries. They exercised a powerful attraction on the surrounding world. Thus it was, for example, that an entire populus lived about the monasteries and participated in the consecration of the monks and nuns: *associates* and *familiars*. On the other hand, we saw that structures formed in civil society as well, as we indicated with chivalry. But all these traditions were inspired by monastic traditions. As a result, fervent laymen for a long time afterward organized their spiritual life along those of religious communities.

But the birth of the lay spirit toward the end of the Middle Ages made it imperative to find Christian traditions of a new type. The double movement we mentioned before asserted itself in new dress. The religious were not content to exercise their influence on the world by a sort of contagion; they went out into the world. They took up certain tasks of the layman to show him how to fulfill them in a Christian way. In the world of the laity, on the other hand, new institutions appeared adapted to the lay life for its own sanctification.

In the Middle Ages, the laity first became autonomous in the world of thought. This happened with the emergence of the universities. It was then that the Friars Preachers played a very important role in the Christianization of secular learning. Recall but the name of Saint Thomas. The Friars Minor followed them along this same path. Together, these mendicant orders contributed to the integration of the lay evangelical movements into the Church and supplied them with authentic

Christian foundations. Even in spite of the orders' influence, some of these movements became heretical.

In the north of Europe, the Dominicans were also the spiritual directors of that original institution of the Beguines. Everywhere, the order of penitents found a new influx of life in the encounter between the enthusiasm for the evangelical life and the appearance of the mendicant orders.

About this same time, new orders were founded to take care of the sick. These were the hospital orders: the Antonians in the Dauphiné, the Order of the Holy Spirit at Montpellier, the Lazarists in the Orient to aid the lepers, the Crozier Fathers to care for sick pilgrims and crusaders. In like manner, laymen assembled around the Hôtels-Dieu in institutions with a type of spiritual life.

The Renaissance and the Reformation accentuated the autonomy of the lay world. Then Saint Ignatius founded the Society of Jesus with all the mobility required to act wherever necessary to consolidate or create religious structures. But the primary work of the Society was teaching. The traditions they established in society were thus all the more solid because they were deeply rooted in the soul of society's youth. Soon the Jesuits consolidated these traditions by instituting the Sodality of the Blessed Virgin. Many other religious societies were founded in this same age and in the following centuries in response to all human needs and conditions. We might characterize these foundations as a sort of religious *avant-garde* coming to the aid of the layman in the world.

On the lay side of the picture, in addition to the guilds and third orders which continued to grow, we must note two original creations. First is the Company of the Blessed Sacrament founded in 1630. Not only did it furnish its members with a frame of life, but—and this is the novelty—it required its members to go into the world and aid all good enterprises and correct social evils. This latter task was not always the most successful. Thus it came to the aid of destitute farmers, organized distributions to the poor, created medical teams, and financed foreign missions. We could mention other more modest enterprises along this same line, which were anticipations of Catholic Action. Such were the societies of the Shoemakers Friars and the Tailors Friars founded by Henri Buch, a simple shoemaker from Luxembourg.

Along a different but no less original line we see the Society of the Heart of Mary which Father de Clorivière founded at the end of the eighteenth century. This was a sort of secular institute before its time. The women who belonged to it took vows, but lived in the world and were employed at lay tasks. Thus the structures which supported their spiritual life were indeed instruments of the consecration of the world for laymen in the world.

In all this, we have been looking at preliminary movements, but we must wait until the twentieth century to see how the true Christian laity took form. Groups of various types appear in the world. Some of these have the spiritual formation and development of their members as their primary goal. In this way, the members become able to exercise an effective many-faceted apostolate. The third orders and analogous groups (like the Jesuit-inspired *Vie Chrétienne* movement or the Legion of Mary) fall into this category. Many of these are now being reactivated. We must add the pious associations, and the other organizations which favor piety through some practice or commitment. They are not to be looked down on though they are less organized and often less active than those we mentioned before. They too contribute to the consecration of the world.

Then come the Catholic Action movements. Though devoted essentially to the apostolate, they did not neglect the spiritual formation of their members. They set out to introduce Christian traditions in the world by exercising an apostolate of the milieu through the milieu, according to this motto: "See, judge, act." The Marian organizations should be added to these. They were recognized by Pope Pius XII as belonging to Catholic Action, but they belong also to the first category. Their Marian devotion gives them the character of a spiritual group.

A third category is that of what are called the "home" movements. They are Christian family organizations which serve not only as a base of operations, but also as a light-giving center for the milieus of all natural life. Some, like the Christian Family Movement, are made up completely of "households" and are centered on a conjugal spirituality. Many groups of the two preceding categories also lean toward familial forms, but do not exclude the membership of individuals. But an extremely important action on the world is carried out by both. For, in this way, Christian structures form in a more organic manner, starting from the fundamental social cell, the family. All human activities are attached to this primary center: cultural, professional, civic, political, international. Thus the consecration of the world is more effectively carried out than by the separate action of husband and wife in associations for men and for women. In the heart of the family Christian initiative takes primary form and establishes an organized life which will then develop in society as a whole. This type seems to be the most original actualization of the lay apostolate in the twentieth century.

All these Christian structures, whether religious in the strict sense or formed in the world especially for laymen, are effective means in the consecration of the world. They give continuity and stability to this consecration. They bring with them activities, observances, ways of acting or *habitus,* a bodily armor which sets the stage for spiritual development. The human mind does not persist continually in the state of clear consciousness; it passes through alternating obscurity and light. But thought is prolonged by action; it is colored by intention. And the intention does not remain exterior to the deed, but it informs it, and gives it its direction, coherence, and unity. These intentions we are now talking about are influenced in great part by all our actions. If these prefigure the city of God, we can see how important lay action is for the consecration of the world.

Nevertheless, we will never reach the end here below. We cannot hope to see the city of God one day established in its perfection in the world. Even the most complete models, such as Benedictine monasteries, are still imperfect. They can never assume the totality of human tasks and integrate them into the monastic city, especially in our day when the expansions of science and technology require means far beyond those of a small city. Even medieval Christianity fell short of realizing the perfect city of God. Despite its harmony, it had many weaknesses that make it somewhat less than the absolute model of Christianity. However, we do not see how the fortunate acquisitions of the modern world can all find a place in its framework.

So the action of the laity should be conceived as a ceaseless effort to construct the Christian world through many attempts repaid by failures as well as by successes. But this work is not in vain. The efficacy of Christ's redemptive sacrifice remains forever. It has a redemptive value, and it is this final aspect of the spirituality of the layman which we must now examine.

FOOTNOTES:
[1] Mk. 9, 5.
[2] Jn. 14, 8.
[3] 2 Cor. 4, 18.
[4] 2 Cor. 5, 1–2.

[5] Cf. Acts 7, 58.

[6] Acts 2, 42; cf. 2, 46–47.

[7] Acts 2, 45–46; cf. 4, 32–35.

[8] Acts 4, 32–33.

[9] Cf. Josef Siegwart, *Die Chorherren und Chorfrauengemeinschaften in der deutschsprachigen Schweiz vom 6. Jht. bis 1160,* Fribourg, 1962.

[10] Cf. G. Meersseman, *Etudes sur les anciennes confréries dominicaines,* Archivum FF. Praedicatorum, 23 (1953), pp. 277–278.

9

Consecration and Redemption in Charity

The spirituality of the layman is a spirituality of commitment to temporal affairs, but these temporal affairs are redeemed by the Cross of Christ. The accent placed on the first point should not keep us from giving the second its important place nor from recognizing that the redemptive mystery everywhere underlies the layman's action in the world. The reparation won by Christ's sacrifice did not, however, void the reality of creation. Therefore, we must develop the perspective in which the layman is to develop his life being conscious of his call to work for the consecration of the world.

The layman will first realize that the work he accomplishes on the temporal plane is fleeting. Temporal values are indeed real, but they are nonetheless in continual danger. The layman engaged in human enterprises experiences this daily. He uses Christian wisdom to discover the limits of human power. Even in the face of the prodigious successes of science and technology, he refuses to give in to rash enthusiasm and to repeat the phrase of Stalin recently affixed to a Russian exposition pavilion: "Science can do all." As far advanced as the calculations of man may be, there is always a failure in the system, a defiance of man's intelligence and will. This reveals his weakness.

Now let us turn to the esthetic values, that domain of beauty, art, letters, and culture where the humanists of all times have found consolation. Whoever knows how to look, finds here another of man's limitations, the instability of the most signal successes. The most beautiful instant passes and nothing can prevent its flight.

The Christian civilization, which the layman strives to construct gradually, rests on these fragile foundations. He must have the courage to admit the possibility of failures and the collapses of even the most promising attempts. Though Christians have experienced discouragement in periods of crisis, this is not the true spirit of Christ. Hear the words of Saint Augustine as he calls upon the Christians frightened by the fall of Rome to the Visigoths in 420: "Arise then, you, the race predestined to heaven! You who as strangers here below seek a fatherland in heaven, you who aspire to communion with the saints and angels, be aware that you have come on earth in order to leave it one day. You cross the world striving toward Him who created the world. Do not be discouraged by those who love this world, and wish to remain here. They will have to leave it whether they want to or not. Do not let yourselves be deceived; do not let yourselves be seduced. These blows— the fall of Rome—are afflictions, not scandals. If you are just, they are trials. Tribulation is what you make it: trial or damnation. As it finds you, such will it be. Tribulation is a fire: if it finds you as gold, it burns out the impurities. If it finds you as straw, it burns you to ashes." [1]

The disruption and split of medieval Christianity by the Reformation was also a scandal for many. These attitudes betray a misunderstanding of the condition of humanity which Christ chose to assume in order to save the world, and in which the disciples had to continue living to apply the fruits of His sacrifice.

To this is added the influence of the forces of evil. Through the fall of Adam, man not only lost the privileges resulting from grace, which placed him in superhuman harmony, but his sin also unleashed anarchic forces in every grade of being, even to the spiritual depths of the universe. The power of the demons is not a myth; it is constantly at work. To be precise, the consecration of the world implies the reconquest of all forces in order to submit them to God. This includes the fallen spiritual powers. But the struggle is long and exacting. There are many failures, alternate successes and reverses, as we strive for the definitive victory at the end of time.

The first duty of the layman in the world is to keep his vision clearly fixed on the real, and to rid himself of any illusion that would falsely embellish reality. His vision, however, should be penetrating enough to discover the true good behind the evil, for hidden values are momentarily dominated by evil motives. No being is pure evil. Inasmuch as a creature has being, it is good. But this being is not stable; it is on the move toward its fulfillment. It must perfect itself and finally become complete. If it seeks what it lacks for perfection in a reality less than itself, a reality which lowers its value, then it becomes perverted and evil. Thus the beauty of the body should lead one to the beauty of the spirit. If the attraction of the senses leads one to be content with mere sensual satisfaction, love is then impossible and all is destroyed.

In the midst of the world corrupted by evil, then, we must free all the forces of good, rescue them from perverse seductions, assume them and give them their genuine fulfillment in their true temporal end. And we must direct this temporal end toward the eternal end, God. Saint Augustine's great passions of love, once redirected and turned toward the Lord, added tremendous generosity to his life of holiness.

The grace of the redemption works this transformation, and it is at the disposal of every Christian. The Son of God descended into human nature; he recreated it. He took upon Himself all evil by taking upon Himself the results of evil, all suffering and death. Jesus took upon Himself this annihilation of being produced by sin, and transformed it by an act of infinite love. An object cut off from God is a negation of being. If the creature seeks its end in a created object, a limited end, it annihilates itself in suffering and death. It was capable of the infinite, but it tried to fulfill its power of the infinite in the very negation of that infinite. This clash between the power of the infinite and the denial of it can produce only suffering and death. Christ redeemed this power of the infinite inscribed in human nature. He infused into it a new and absolute love. In a ransom painful to the created, this love takes on suffering and death to offer a totally disinterested gift to God and thus reenter the divine circuit of love. This consequent pain, caused by the ransom of the being from its own annihilation, becomes the condition and means of a complete ransoming from self for a pure giving of self to another, to the God of love.

Through this transfiguration of suffering, Christ made the evil of sin the occasion for a greater flow of love in the world. For love has an end in view, the perfect union of the lovers in the reciprocal giving of self. Love is not entirely pure unless the gift of self is absolute and without reserve. But in the heart of the man who gives himself, there is the danger of a subtle egotism, an intimate satisfaction at being the giver. Then the love is no longer pure, the giving is no longer total, for there is no longer the complete forgetfulness of self. But in suffering, these withdrawals into self become impossible. All that remains is the pure ardor of generosity toward the other. Thus Christ, assuming the suffering resulting from sin, realized more than a simple reparation. His was a renewal, for He made human nature share the perfect love of the Son of God.[2]

We too, through redemptive suffering in union with Christ's love, fulfill the task of consecrating the world. In his efforts to sanctify every creature and bring it into the divine mystery in the Mass, the layman clashes with evil both within and without himself. He will be tempted to discouragement before this task which he must continually take up. But he discovers a new means of success by sharing in the redemption of Christ through suffering. Man with creation is to share in the divine mystery, and this mystery is essentially a society united in love. Normally, all the activity of creatures communicates this spiritual love. The various gradations of being contain a prefiguration of it, and as one ascends the scale of beings, this union in diversity becomes more perfect. The instrument which communicates charity then is in harmony with the deep spiritual current it communicates. But the instrument has been broken by sin; success seems impossible. Then we must remember that the divine love is given from on high. It is so lofty and so transcends every creature that the perfection of the instrument is of little concern. In the order of redemption, charity breaks through the broken instrument. In spite of the fracture, and even because of it, the breakthrough is all the more intense. The gash of sin in no way interrupts the flood of divine love.

Thus the layman follows the course of men to introduce divine life into the world and to draw the world into the divine mystery for consecration. But the moment comes when he clashes with suffering. It is an invitation to take the short road by despoiling himself and in pain ransoming creation. At this moment, he can but let himself be totally embraced by charity. Up to now, he strove to communicate the flame of holocaust to the pyre that it might mount as an offering to God. But, suddenly, the fire of heaven has come down on the altar and all is consumed.

Union with the redemptive sacrifice of Christ makes this possible, for it allows us to participate in His perfect act of love which has assumed all suffering. Once again we must underline the role of the layman in the sacrifice of the Mass, and recall again the sacraments, instruments of grace, placed at his disposal. Amid the human roles the layman assumes in this manner, we must pay special attention to those which imply suffering. He can repeat in his turn the words of Saint Paul: "What is lacking of the suffering of Christ, I fill up in my flesh for His body, which is the Church." [3]

The last part of the Apostle's text opens even more vast perspectives. Each Christian is a bearer of the whole Church and is responsible for the salvation of the entire world. Charity gives him the power to extend this redemptive effectiveness beyond the narrow confines of his habitual relationships to the extremities of the earth. In fact, the charity in which the layman lives the divine life is the love of friendship which effects the unity of the lovers, God and His children. Each person is a center loved by God who stirs up this life of charity in it, and at the same time a center from which love sets out to be carried to each of the persons of this society.

Each Christian, because he is a member of this immense Mystical Body of Christ, can take on himself the evils which afflict the body and which are an obstacle to its harmonious perfection. He surrounds them with charity from the heart of Christ; in Christ he reforms the wounded creatures. Even if the evil seems still to subsist on the temporal and visible plane, in the reality of God's mystery all is made valuable and will bear fruit a hundredfold for those now in privation and suffering. To the measure in which a single Christian has charity and, in prayer united to Christ's offering Himself in sacrifice, carries his intention to some other part of the Mystical Body, all the value veiled and turned aside by evil begins to free itself, to stir, and to develop. The source of charity stirred in each one by the love of Christ also taps all that flood of grace which springs up secretly in all parts of the world throughout time and space.

This charity should be deep-rooted in the condition of humanity. A vague imagination accompanied by emotional feelings is not enough. If the love of friendship is a true community of all things among those who love, the Christian cannot effectively assume the misery of another and bring forth the good in it unless he enters personally into the mystery of suffering. This is only to follow Christ, who took upon Himself the condition of humanity to effect the renewal of salvation. The Christian must then accept the sacrifices he meets in his own life in order to bear the suffering of his brother whose name he perhaps does not know, nor the place where he lives. He will not undergo the same suffering materially, but he will participate in the same mystery of suffering common to all.

In this we see that the task of redemption does not fall less lightly on the layman, nor is his task less effective than that of those on a high rung in the hierarchy of the Church. What counts here is not dignity, but the intensity of charity. Perhaps he who is in the world can see more clearly the misery in the world. He hears more clearly the appeal for salvation raised by suffering humanity. This quality is the most ennobling characteristic of the spirituality of the layman.

FOOTNOTES:

[1] *Sermon,* 81, 7.

[2] We developed this theme in the collective work *Souffrance, valeur chrétienne,* under the title: *Le Mystère de la souffrance et le don de l'amour,* Tournai: Casterman, 1957, pp. 205–223.

[3] Col. 1, 24.

10

The Role of the Layman
in the Mystical Body [1]

At the beginning of the book, we could have started out by defining the role of the layman in the Mystical Body, but an *a priori* method might have separated us from reality. We preferred to describe first the life of the layman as it should be in the Church. It is now easier to come to the final precisions.

Our starting point is the primary fact of the constitution of the body of the Church in which all Christians have a part regardless of rank.

In the course of His earthly mission, Christ gathered a number of disciples about Him. They did not come to Him by chance. He chose [2] them and He would send them to the world: "Go, therefore, and make disciples of all nations, baptizing them in the name of the Father, and of the Son, and of the Holy Spirit." [3] They were to spread the Good News, not in their own name, but on behalf of the Lord; they were to communicate the divine life whose source is Jesus Christ. They were not acting as isolated individuals. All together were one with Christ. In Him, with Him, and through Him they were but one being, one living body: "I am the vine, you are the branches. He who abides in Me, and I in him, he bears much fruit; for without Me you can do nothing." [4]

In the course of time, the community of the disciples grew considerably. Yet, whatever the number or time, each of the disciples was a part of the living body; no one could remain outside. The withered branch is cut off and cast far from the vine. [5]

. Today, as then, every Christian shares in the life of the Mystical Body of Christ, the Church. This means that he not only has a place in the body, but that he takes an active part in the vital exchanges within the body and in its exterior growth. According to Saint Paul, he is to "practice the truth in love, and so grow up in all things in Him who is the head, Christ. For from him the whole body (being closely joined and knit together through every joint of the system according to the functioning in due measure of each single part) derives its increase to the building up of itself in love." [6]

This elementary participation in the life of the Church belongs to all by virtue of their incorporation into Christ through Baptism. This is not yet the place to distinguish the categories of the faithful, whether laymen or clerics. On this level, the layman has no special role in the Church.

But from another point of view, the Mystical Body does have structures in which we can discover the foundations of the role proper to the layman. Certainly each member is responsible for the life of the entire body, but each has his own place according to his rank. "God has set the members, each of them, in the body as He willed. Now if they were all one member, where would the body be?" [7]

From the earliest times, the Church has appeared in the form of a body. Christ immediately determined the essential functions in His Church. With time and growth of the Church, and under the inspiration of the Holy Spirit manifested through various events, new specifications were made. These specifications were a part of the manifestations of the Holy Spirit which Christ promised that night in the Cenacle: "But the Advocate, the Holy Spirit, whom the Father will send in My name, He will teach you all things." [8]

In this same manner, Jesus gave Peter a preeminence over the other apostles: "Thou art Peter, and upon this rock I will build My Church." [9] He renewed this after the Resurrection: "Simon, son of John, dost thou love Me?" He asked. And He followed the affirmative answer with: "Feed My sheep." [10]

In the early Church, certain tasks which the apostles at first took on were given to lesser ministers, deacons set aside to "serve at tables." They then selected "seven men of good reputation, full of the Spirit and of wisdom," to put in charge of this work. "And after they (the apostles) had prayed, they laid their hands upon them." [11]

On the other hand, Saint Paul simply mentions a certain number of functions and "charisms" as if they were known facts: "And God indeed has placed some in the Church, first apostles, secondly prophets, thirdly teachers; after that miracles, then gifts of healing, services of help, power of administration, and the speaking of various tongues." [12] We begin to see a certain hierarchy among the faithful gifted with these talents. According to the text cited, some are *placed* in the Church by God: apostles, prophets, and teachers. Father Allo says "This triad became the teaching force of the Church." [13] Other Christians have gifts which are not officially designated by the Church. Among others, the gift of tongues, an impulse of the soul, manifested exteriorly by a kind of mysterious language incomprehensible without an interpreter. Of course this charism has to be controlled; this role seems to fall to the prophet as the text leads us to believe.[14]

So we recognize, besides the activities each member can exercise in the Church, functions which are proper to certain members who are directors of the community.

In time, the hierarchical structure of the community becomes more clear. The need arose to formulate this more specifically. There were already terms to designate the directors of the Church, a terminology which dates back to the beginnings. The problem was to find terms to designate those who did not belong to special categories which implied an official function. What vocabulary should the Church adopt to permit her to assemble and embrace in a single view the complex of the Church's structure?

A suitable vocabulary already existed in the Greek language. It needed only to be adapted to ecclesiastical terminology. This was done around the third century of the Christian era. It was then that the word *layman* came into use to designate the faithful who received no consecration to a special function.

How was this word *layman* chosen and spread? [15]

Some insist that layman comes from the Greek *laos,* and means the people of God or consecrated people. However, this explanation has no historical foundation in the Church's history. Also it has the grave disadvantage of basing the consecration of the layman on purely sociological reality.

The fact is that the word *layman* was taken from the language of Greek literature and little by little introduced into ecclesiastical language with the connotation of an *unconsecrated* object or being.

At the beginning of Greek literature, the word *laos* designated the people in general or even the mass of the population as distinguished from their leaders. This same word was also used with regard to religious worship; it then meant the people who came to be present at the worship. The adjective derived from it, *laicos,* preserves this relative meaning. We find it in the third century B.C. with the meaning: "who belong to the population of the country, distinguished from the official administration."

These terms are always used with such a connotation in the Greek translations of the Bible. The Septuagint version, begun around the end of the fourth century B.C. at Alexandria, uses *laos* to designate the people of Israel as distinguished from the pagan nations (*ethne*), and even more often the masses of the people as opposed to their leaders and especially to the ministers of the Temple, the priests and levites. For example, in the book of Nehemias in the question of the return of the Jews to Jerusalem we find the words: "And the priests, and the levites . . . and the rest of the common people . . . dwelt in their cities." [16] The same is used in the prophetic text of Isaias [17] announcing that Yahweh will disperse the inhabitants, "layman and priest alike, servant and master." In Jeremias we find numerous texts making this same distinction. For example, he speaks of "a prophet or a priest or anyone else." [18] And again: "Now the priests, the prophets, and all the people heard Jeremias speak these words." [19] In 29,1 we read: "This is the contents of the letter which the prophet Jeremias sent from Jerusalem to the remaining elders among the exiles, to the priests, the prophets, and all the people." [20]

Later, other Jewish translators used the word *laos* and its derivative *laicos*. In the second century A.D. we find it in Aquila, Symmachus, and Theodotion. Thus when David was fleeing and asked food of Achimelech the priest, he replied: "I have no common (*laicos*) bread at hand, but only holy bread." [21] The same is used by Symmachus and Theodotion in Ezechiel 48,15, and by Theodotion alone in Ezechiel 22,16.

These classifications had been adopted, and the Christians in their turn utilized them by adapting them to the structure of the Church. We find witnesses of this from the third century on. Thus writes Clement of Rome: "Special functions have been conferred upon the high priest, the priests, and the levites; special places were marked out for the priests; to the levites fell the services proper; the laymen were bound by the precepts familiar to laymen." [22] This is a triple division analogous to that of Ezechiel. Clement of Alexandria adapted the classification even more and distinguished "priests, deacons, and laymen." [23] Finally, Origen opposes the term layman to cleric, priest and deacon. [24]

From now on this will be the fundamental meaning of the word layman: he who has not received a special consecration in the Church, or he whose relative position to that of consecrated persons is that these latter play the role among the laymen of Christ's instruments to procure for them certain graces of light and life.

It is only in most recent religious literature that the layman and the consecrated have been identified. We believe this is a source of confusion and see in it no basis for defining the role of the layman. But, if we preserve the traditional terminology, all becomes clear. It remains for us to show this.

Let us begin with the meaning of the word *layman*. The layman is first of all he who, though all the while part of the Church, has not received a special consecration making him capable of exercising the hierarchical priesthood. Laymen are the people in the Church.

But how are they part of the people? Are they not just the mass of men, a flock that can only receive passively? Certainly not. At the beginning of the chapter, we recalled that every member of the Church is active. The simple Christian has received a character enabling him to exercise an active part in the Church. He too has received a certain consecration.

However, his consecration does not result from his belonging to the people of the Church. That would be a purely sociological basis, as if Christ had assembled men about Him and imposed upon them the designation of holy people, lay people. The powers given to the leaders would then be an addition, without being an integral part of the structure of the Church. In reality, the constitution of the Church is very different. Each of the faithful is plunged into Christ. And since all form but one Christ, whom all have put on to the very depths of their being, they form a single living body. This body is structured so as to form a real organism. The directive organs effectively signify Christ's mediation by bringing light and life to the totality of the body. And the part of the body receptive of grace is formed by the laymen. The Christian who has not received the special consecration giving him a directive function in the body, has his own role, that of the layman. But the first degree of consecration remains his; it gives him his dignity; it truly permits him to live the life of the Mystical Body. The Christian is not consecrated because he is a layman, but on the contrary, he is, in his role of layman, also consecrated. The laity is not the source of his consecration; it is the category in which he must be placed because of his role in the Church and in the world. He receives his consecration from another source. So we must seek out other words than that of *layman* if we wish to recall the source of this consecration and the active role the laymen too must play in the Church.

On the other hand, every faithful lives in the world where he is to act as a leaven of life and salvation. But the Christians who have received the special consecration, conferring on them a directive function in the Church, are to confine themselves to this function, devote themselves to it, and this implies a special separation from the world. It follows that the unconsecrated, the layman, will find himself alone fully situated in the world. His particular role in the Church, not engaged in a special way in the eucharistic mystery or the ministry of the word, gives him consequently a special role in the world, implying a personal engagement in the world's affairs.)

We can recall here the schema already used in chapter four: (The sacrifice of Christ is at the center of the Church; then come the priests, charged with re-presenting this sacrifice and communicating its fruits everywhere and always; finally, at the periphery are the laymen engaged in the world but not of the world.)

(The priests are set apart, specially consecrated to accomplish their ministry) The layman constantly breathes, in a way, the grace diffused by the sacerdotal ministry; completely receptive, he is all the while active with constant apostolic zeal to utilize in the best way possible this grace of salvation for himself and for others. So(through all his earthly tasks, the layman is constantly working for the consecration of the world to God.)

From this first point of view, then, (the layman, placed in his relationship with the priesthood as *unconsecrated* in the strict sense, still enjoys an active participation in the sacrifice of Christ and is thus linked to the priesthood in such a way as to enter actively into the eucharistic mystery.) If then we use the word layman to distinguish him clearly from the priest, we must recognize that, in his role as layman, he is gifted with a positive content which makes him worthy of the name of *faithful* of Christ, *Christian, "other Christ."* This positive content does not come from a so-called participation in the laity, but from the *character of Baptism,* and is matured by that of Confirmation. This character configures every Christian to Christ, whatever his place in the hierarchy of the Church, and gives him a primary share in the priesthood of Christ.[25]

However, we must take note of a second point of view.(The consecration of the world, which the layman is to accomplish, is not extrinsic to the realities of this world.) It must permeate to the point where these creatures are again directed toward

God as a continual offering of praise and reparation, a continual thanksgiving and sacrifice. This again concerns Christ's sacrifice, for these offerings are united to Christ's that He may transform them and make them part of His own sacrifice. The creatures thus consecrated take on a *religious value*. And among these creatures thus sanctified, the most important is man, the layman himself.

Nevertheless, the task of consecration is never completed here below; thus the layman is on the move toward this total consecration of his own existence, but he is not yet perfect, and so a part of his interior or exterior being remains worldly, belonging yet to the secular. On the other hand, there are those who have already arrived at this perfection *in voto* by "vows." These, through the special mercy of God, have obtained a mysterious transfer to perfection thanks to a total commitment of their will to God. These are called *religious*. With regard to this absolute end, the layman is yet *unconsecrated* (i.e., not totally consecrated). The term layman then situates the Christian in relation to that magnetic pole, the religious life.

But this purely negative meaning requires a positive content. For though the layman is not totally consecrated, he aspires with his whole being to this total belonging. Even more, he already has in himself, in potency and in act, all the powers to be one day perfectly exercised; he has received Christ into himself, or rather, he has put on Christ, he has been buried in Him. Finally, he is one of the *baptized,* plunged into the death of Christ to rise again with Him. Though completely distinguished from the *religious,* the layman shares in the religious life; and the presence of religious in the Mystical Body is a testimony as well as a constant and effective appeal to draw all other members to total consecration.

But once again, it is not by virtue of participating in the laity that the layman tends toward the total consecration to the Lord. It is in virtue of his *Baptism* which plants in his soul the seed of total consecration and enables him to march toward perfection in the very situation (or framework) of the laity.

When the term layman is made thus precise, we can then accurately locate him in the living body of Christ and, by the same token, we see his place in the grand redemptive movement which leads all creation between the two poles of this mystery, his place in relation to Christ, the Alpha and the Omega, the beginning and the end.

He is first of all a layman, that is, he takes part in the world which has become profane, having lost its primitive consecration through sin; but he receives the grace of salvation flowing constantly from the redemptive sacrifice of Christ through the ministry of the priest. His attitude is not one of hostility to the divine world; he is a part of the people who actively receive the mystery of salvation. He preserves in his heart a profound respect for God, a sense of the transcendence of God over the creature, especially the sinful creature.

In spite of the grace of salvation, he remains a layman too because he still belongs to this world, and this world is profane inasmuch as it has not totally been consecrated to Christ and has not yet come to a perfect identification with the kingdom of God. But his interior attitude is that of the Christian who awaits the return of the Lord, eager for His coming and striving more and more to direct all toward Him.

From the point of view of God's transcendence, there always exists an abyss between the layman and the Lord, His creator. But from the point of view of the consecration, this abyss is progressively filled until unity with the Lord is attained, and this is the last end.

The life of the layman, that is of the simple Christian or

baptized, is thus admirably conformed to the words of Christ: "in the world but not of the world." [26] So too is his interior apostolic activity in conformity with Saint Paul's words: "using the world as though not using it." [27] So too, finally, the ideal he strives to realize is that which the Apostle also proposes: "All things are yours (yes, all this profane world, this world fallen and separated from God in which you are engaged) but you are Christ's and Christ is God's." [28]

FOOTNOTES:

[1] The essentials of this chapter appeared in the January 1962 number of *Vie dominicaine,* Fribourg, pp. 3–10. Meanwhile, Father E. Schillebeeckx published in *Tijdschrift voor theologie,* 3, 1962, the excellent article "Dogmatiek van ambt en lekestaat" (pp. 258–292), which comes to the point of this question exactly. We feel quite in accord with his article. (See our article in *La Vie spirituelle,* March 1963, pp. 358–367.)

[2] Cf. Jn. 15, 16.

[3] Mt. 28, 19.

[4] Jn. 15, 5.

[5] Cf. Jn. 15, 6.

[6] Eph. 4, 15–16.

[7] I Cor. 12, 18–19.

[8] Jn. 14, 26.

[9] Mt. 16, 18.

[10] Jn. 21, 15–17.

[11] Acts 6, 3–6.

[12] I Cor. 12, 28.

[13] E. B. Allo, *Saint Paul, première Epître aux Corinthiens,* Paris, 1934, p. 336.

[14] I Cor. 14, 26–33.

[15] See the well-documented article of I. de la Potterie, "L'origine et le sens primitif du mot 'laïc' " *Nouvelle Revue Théologique,* 80 (1958), pp. 840–853.

[16] Neh. 7, 73.

[17] Is. 24, 2.

[18] Jer. 23, 34.

[19] Jer. 26, 7; and Jer. 26, 11.

[20] Cf. also Jer. 36, 9.

[21] 1 Sm. 21, 4, the same in all three versions.

[22] XL, 6.

[23] *Strom.*, III, 12, 90, I; *P.G.*, 8, 1189 *C*.

[24] *P.G.*, 13, 369 *C–D*.

[25] The terminology we here propose accords exactly with the doctrinal exposé of the pastoral letter of the Most Rev. Emile-Joseph de Smedt, Bishop of Bruges, published under the title: *Le Sacerdoce des fidèles* (Desclée de Brouwer, 1961); note especially n. 1 on p. 115.

[26] Jn. 17, 11–14.

[27] 1 Cor. 7, 21.

[28] 1 Cor. 3, 22.

Conclusion: Participation in the Mission of the Church

Every Christian, whether cleric, religious, or layman, lives the divine life communicated to the body of Christ. Like every member of the body, the layman shares in the exchanges within the life of Christ and the mystery of the Trinity. He shares also in the growth of the body which is developing in the world and assimilating all the good it finds until the fulfillment of the "last days." In all this there is nothing to distinguish his spiritual life from that of all Christians.

But, for the layman, this life has its own coloring because of his role in the body of the world. First, he is a representative of the hierarchy. The laity constitute the people of God who, through the instrumentality of the leaders appointed by Christ, receive the word of God and the life flowing from the sacrifice of Calvary. On the other hand, being free of all responsibility in the directive tasks of the Church, the layman is in a position of special commitment in the world. It is in view of this double perspective that he participates in the common life of the Church. He has experience proper to this double role, and with it he enriches the entire body of the Church and uses grace and other helps given by the Church to better answer the needs of his situation. Thus he comes to God along a road suited to his vocation and characterized by his role as a layman in the Church and in the world. According to these facts, we have to recognize a spirituality which is proper to the layman.

The layman has his own part to play in the mission of the Church. Her mission is his concern, for the Church is not made up of a head alone. She is a living body, and each layman is a member just as is the cleric and the religious. Whatever affects the Church, affects him according to his place within her.

The Church received a mission: this means that she is sent. Christ is the one who sends her. Her mission is rooted in the mission of Christ, and continues that mission: "As the Father has sent Me, so also I send you." [1] And so the Church pursues the mission of salvation. The disciples of Christ, each in his turn, must announce and apply to the world the redemptive mystery which Christ came to announce and accomplish. All people are to be gathered in: "Go, therefore, and make disciples of all nations, baptizing them in the name of the Father, and of the Son, and of the Holy Spirit." [2]

The area is immense; the people of the world are innumerable. Not only must the disciples bring them a message, but they must make that message a leaven in their lives. The members of the Church who are the most committed to the life of the world will be especially effective in fulfilling this mission. They are the great *avant-garde* of the Church; they are responsible for its growth in the world. So the layman should consider himself as sent to go ahead with vigor, to utilize all his activities as instruments of the redemption.

Yet nobody has a mission unless somebody sends him. The layman too should recognize the source of his mission. The Church has been sent by Christ, and Christ, the Son of God, the Word eternally begotten of the Father, sends the Church from the very heart of the Trinity. Now the mission cannot be truly accomplished without perfect fidelity to the one who sends. The Church maintains this fidelity through the inspiration of the Holy Spirit, who keeps it on the right road. Let the layman remember that he is a member of the Church, and that only through the Church does he receive light and life. While going ahead in the milieu of the world, he remains bound to the truth and to the source of life through his fidelity to the leaders of the Church.

And now, if we desire a guide and model of this fidelity, we need only turn our eyes toward the heart of the Church, to the perfect model of fidelity, the Blessed Virgin Mary. For the layman, this especially will be the meaning of Marian devotion: to seek Mary's inspiration to conduct his life obediently in his layman's mission according to the will of God.

Thus the spirituality of the layman finds a fulfillment in his mission. It develops him from two poles: the Church who is one with Christ, and the world to be saved. The misery of the world, which the layman experiences more than anyone else, is constantly calling to him and makes his apostolate challenging. But he remains firm, attached to the Lord, inseparable from Him in His Church. And here he finds the inexhaustible source of life and the final end of all action.

FOOTNOTES:

[1] Jn. 20, 21.

[2] Mt. 28, 19.

Selected Bibliography

Bouyer, Louis, *Introduction to Spirituality* (New York: Desclée, 1961); *id., Christian Initiation* (New York: Macmillan, 1960)

Boylan, M. Eugene, O.C.R., *This Tremendous Lover* (Westminster, Md.: Newman, 1957)

Chautard, J. C., *The Soul of the Apostolate* (New York: Kenedy, 1937)

Davis, Charles, *Liturgy and Doctrine* (London: Sheed, 1960)

de Fabrègues, Jean, *Christian Marriage,* in *Twentieth Century Encyclopedia of Catholicism* (New York: Hawthorn, 1959)

Howell, Clifford, *Of Sacraments and Sacrifice* (Collegeville, Minn.: Liturgical Press, 1952)

Leclercq, Jacques, *Christians in the World* (New York: Sheed, 1961)

Martimort, Aimé-Georges, *The Signs of the New Covenant* (Collegeville, Minn.: Liturgical Press, 1963)

Meyer, Bernard F., *Lend Me Your Hands* (Chicago: Fides, 1955)

Perrin, Joseph, *Christian Perfection and Married Life* (Westminster, Md.: Newman, 1958); *id., Secular Institutes; Consecration to God and Life in the World* (New York: Kenedy, 1961)

Schillebeeckx, Edward H., *Vatican II, The Struggle of Minds and Other Essays*—includes the essay *The Layman in the Church*

(Dublin: Gill and Son, 1963); *id., Christ: Sacrament of the Encounter with God* (New York: Sheed, 1963)

Suenens, L. J. Cardinal, *The Theology of the Apostolate* (Chicago: Regnery, 1955)

Suhard, Emmanuel Cardinal, *The Church Today, Growth or Decline?* (Notre Dame, Ind.: Fides, 1948)

Thils, Gustave, *Christian Holiness* (Tielt, Belgium: Lannoo, 1961)

Trese, Leo, *Many Are One* (Chicago: Fides, 1952)